BRIGHTER ...

FOR BRIGHT YOUNG PEOPLE
WHO ALREADY KNOW SOME

by

Harry Thompson Russell
[H—T—R—]

BRIGHTER FRENCH SERIES : VOLUME I

PHÆTON
PUBLISHING LTD.
—— Dublin ——

BRIGHTER FRENCH

[FIRST PUBLISHED OCTOBER 1927, LONDON]
THIS NEW EDITION PUBLISHED IN 2010
BY PHAETON PUBLISHING LIMITED, DUBLIN

Original (1927) text by Harry Thompson RUSSELL
© Anne ASTON
Original (1927) cover drawing & illustrations
© estate of Eric FRASER

Biographies of H.T. RUSSELL & Eric FRASER:
© 2010 S–J–.
Compilation © 2010: Phaeton Publishing Ltd.
Book design © 2010:
O'Dwyer & Jones Design Partnership

*British Library Cataloguing In Publication
Data: a catalogue record for this book
is available from the British Library*

Printed and bound in the U.K.
Third impression 2012
ISBN: 978-0-9553756-7-5   PAPERBACK

THE SEARCH FOR H—T—R—
HARRY THOMPSON RUSSELL

A DRAWING OF a scantily-clad 1920s nightclub dancer and a promise of *'colloquial and idiomatic French for Bright Young People (who already know some)'* were on the jacket. Inside was text that was racy and politically incorrect, but flawless in grammar and subtlety of usage.

It was a volume that could have been produced only in the age of cocktails and jazz, and the original 1927 edition of *Brighter French* had the look of a time-travelling flapper—still partying—when the publishers spotted it in a stack of dry, academic texts at a university book sale.

Should you ever need to say in French:

> True, I've never seen her spit in the cups or blow her nose on the table napkins, but she looks just the kind that would—

or

> He did indeed do a cure at Vichy, but it seems he persisted in mixing the beneficent water with whiskey. So, there was no improvement, but rather the reverse—

or (included for the virtuous purpose of illustrating the historical present tense)

> He comes back one day and is quite aghast to find she has very calmly taken on another fellow—

this is the only text that will help you.

It was a book that had to be republished,

but there was one big problem: who was the author? In the original edition, the author's name was given mysteriously only as 'H–T–R–,' with address 'London' in 1927 (and 'Montpellier' in a follow-up book published in 1932).

It emerged that the publishers were not the first to wonder about the identity of the author. In 1927, when *Brighter French* first came out, there had been much speculation about who H–T–R– was. By 1932 the still mysterious author was acknowledging (in idiomatic French, of course) that the racy style of his books had given rise to the impression (mistaken, he insisted) that H–T–R– was a rake:

> C'est une légende erronée, quoique *au demeurant* assez flatteuse !
> —This idea, though possibly flattering, is quite incorrect.

Half a century later, his identity remained the subject of conjecture. In 1980, for instance, *Teach Yourself French* (36th impression) referred in its Preface to '…that brilliant anonymous volume *Brighter French*…' (before adding regretfully that, by then, it might only be found in libraries).

So who was H–T–R– and what had become of him? Before his identity was established, a lot of helpful people had become as curious as the publishers.

The search started in the British Library,

which was able to provide his full name: Harry (or Henry) Thompson Russell, born 1875. The library had no other information about him however, and did not know the date or the place of his death.

The publishers of the original edition (Geoffrey Bles, Pall Mall) had long ago been taken over by Harper Collins, who helpfully looked into their records, but had no information to offer.

The name, Harry Russell, made the search more difficult. The British Isles are filled with men of that name (many of them born in the same year as H–T–R–).

The search then turned to Montpellier and the *département* of Hérault, where obliging officials (and householders) looked through their archives, but no official record of Harry could be found. An ingenious suggestion however by the British Consul, Norman Paget, brought the search to Strathclyde University, where archivist Margaret Harrison found a letter written by H–T–R– among the papers of Sir Patrick Geddes. Dated 1931, it was an acceptance of a job offered to him by Geddes to teach French at the Scots College in Montpellier. Unfortunately, this job would not last long. Geddes was to die the following year, and his *Collège des Écossais* would die with him.

The Montpellier trail had gone cold, so the search turned back to the British Library, where

J. D. Jenkins of the Humanities Reference Service came up with further clues.

The same H. T. Russell (in 1902-4) had published various army manuals and (as Captain H.T. Russell, R.F.A., in 1905) a French-English Military Vocabulary, which included such invaluable expressions as:

He had the whole Zulu army down upon him.

— *Il avait toute l'armée zulu sur les bras.*

The Archduke passed all his troops over the Adige.

— *L'archiduc fit traverser l'Adige à toutes ses troupes.*

The Catalogue of the War Office Library indicated that he had been in the Royal Artillery, so the search moved on to the Royal Artillery Museum in Woolwich. It was only then that a H–T–R– began to emerge who was very different from the personality the publishers had been imagining. The seeming *boulevardier* had another side.

As a professional soldier, H–T–R– had enjoyed a distinguished military career. He had served in two wars (he was mentioned in Despatches in the second South African War, and advanced to the rank of Brevet Lieut. Colonel in World War I) and was a recognised military analyst in peacetime. Between 1902 and 1905, the military manuals he had published included: *The Employment of Artillery in the Field*; *Practical Gunnery*; *Notes on Strategy & Military History*; and *A French-English*

Military Vocabulary (quoted from above). In 1911, he had won the prestigious Royal United Service Institution Gold Medal (and the first Trench-Gascoigne Prize of Thirty Guineas) for the Military Essay of 1911 (published in 1912), the set topic of which was far removed from *Brighter French*:

THE BEST NATIONAL SYSTEM FOR PROVIDING THE NECESSARY MILITARY FORCE: (i) TO SECURE THE SAFETY OF THE UNITED KINGDOM ON LAND; (ii) TO SUPPORT THE DEFENCE OF THE EMPIRE; (iii) TO ASSIST IN MAINTAINING THE BALANCE OF POWER IN EUROPE.

Extracts from that formidably-titled essay are reproduced here because—unbelievably for such a topic—they are entertaining. Following is Captain Russell's explanation of why the existence of a large middle class made it impractical for the military to rely on volunteers alone:

Most aristocracies can be relied upon to furnish a respectable quota of enthusiasts for the commissioned ranks. In some countries, and particularly in Great Britain, the lower social orders furnish a quota which is surprisingly large in view of their normal conditions of existence, which scarcely make for patriotic enthusiasm...

In all countries, however, the *bourgeoisie* is, of all classes, the most obdurate in regard to military service, and furnishes the fewest volunteer recruits. The *bon bourgeois*, engrossed in business,

in the daily struggle for respectability, overborne
by the devouring Moloch of retail trade, the first
to feel the pinch of taxation in peace, the first
to feel the economic effects of war, the principal
sufferer in unsuccessful war, is commonly an
anti-militarist at heart, an opponent of Forward
Policies, an opportunist, a firm believer in
compromise, a sentimentalist on the subject of
bloodshed, distrustful of everything included in
the word 'discipline,' and oblivious to the stern
necessities of warlike preparation and training.

Nevertheless, the *bon bourgeois*, in the aggregate,
is numerically, politically and economically the
mainstay of the State, and any military system
which fails to obtain from him personal service is
foredoomed to failure.

'Destitution,' on the other hand, in Captain
Russell's opinion, had proved to be a reliable
provider of recruits for the military:

The duress of the empty stomach, the family
quarrel, the unfortunate love-affair, the initial
escapade involving undesirably close contact with
the majesty of the Law, combine to furnish the
majority of recruits, who, needless to say, are
attracted rather by the door of the cook-house
than by the glory of the regimental colours, and
that usually at a tender age.

Also from the Royal Artillery Museum's
librarian, Paul Evans, the publishers learned that
Brevet Lieut. Colonel Harry T. Russell R.A.

had died in Trowbridge, Wiltshire, in 1953. With that information—and through the efforts of many helpful people in Trowbridge (and the *Wiltshire Times*)—the publishers made contact with H–T–R–'s granddaughter, Anne Aston, to whom they are very grateful for her permission to republish his remarkable books.

It was from Mrs Aston that the Irish publishers received the most surprising information of all: the H–T–R– they had been pursuing around England and France had, in fact, come from Ireland.

His family had arrived in Limerick as Anglo-Norman military settlers. The earliest traceable direct ancestor was an 'officer of troops' of an English Parliamentarian army, who was killed in the 1650 siege of Limerick when the city was taken by that army. In the 18th and 19th centuries, many of Harry's direct ancestors held the post of Sheriff of Limerick.

The Russell name is said to have come from Normandy (derived from the name du Rozel or Rosel, according to a family document) and the family maintained strong links with France: around the time of the French Revolution, Harry's great-grand-uncle Dr William Russell is reported to have saved from the guillotine the Comtesse Letellier, whom he later married, settling with her in Toulouse. Prior to World War I, Harry, too, had been living in France.

Harry and his two younger brothers had been sent from Limerick to school in England, at Cheltenham College, where Harry (pictured  left) won a place on the school's rugby team in 1891, and distinguished himself academically, being consistently at or near the top of his class in French, Latin, German (and overall). In 1892, aged 17, he won the Hornby prize for French, and in the same year he joined the British Army as a Royal Artillery cadet. He advanced to 2nd  Lieutenant in 1894 (pictured right in his 'fighting uniform'), to full Lieutenant in 1897, and to Captain in 1901.

His service in the second South African War (from 1899 to 1901) is recorded as follows in the 1911 *Cheltenham College Register*:

> … on the Staff. Relief of Ladysmith, including actions at Spion Kop and Vaal Kranz; operations on Tugela Heights and actions at Pieters Hill; operations in Natal and in the Transvaal (mentioned in Despatches, Queen's Medal with four clasps).

In 1902 he married Alicia Studdert of Bunratty Castle in County Clare, and they had four children. In 1910 he left the army, lived in

Cork, Ireland, and in Dinard, Brittany, but was recalled for service in World War I. Of his service in that war, the 1927 *Cheltenham College Register* records:

> …Imp. Gen. Staff, War Office; Military Operations Directorate, 31 July 1914–Feb. 1919 (Brevet-Major, Brevet-Lieut.-Col., Order of St Anne of Russia).

Harry Thompson Russell led a life of two distinct halves. By the mid-1920s, his marriage to Alicia had ended in a divorce, and Harry's connection with his old life ended. He remarried soon after (to Marion Lee, of County Dublin). Unusually for a marriage between two Irish people in those days, Harry was a Protestant and Marion was a Catholic.

Correspondence of the time indicates that Harry was cut off financially from his family in Ireland after the divorce. His father died in Limerick in 1926. The family home Milford House (rear facade shown right, in its current use as a nursing home and hospice run by Catholic nuns, the Little Company of Mary)  was sold, and the proceeds were divided among Harry's three younger siblings. Harry's younger brother Reginald believed that the sale of the house ended the family's links with Ireland. The Irish War of Independence had ended only five years earlier, and in the 1920s many families who had first come to Ireland as military settlers did leave. His thoughts at the time regarding the sale of the house were recorded in a family history: Reginald 'was regretfully compelled by circumstances of politics and finance to sell Milford House and settle in England thus breaking the last link of the long family connection with Ireland.' (In fact, in the 1940s and 1950s, two of Harry's children would return to live in Ireland.)

Left without family money after the divorce, H–T–R– was resourceful in making a living. In one of the livelier turns of his colourful life, he and his new wife worked as private detectives in London in the 1920s.

Grosvenor 2794.

Lieut. Colonel H. T. Russell,
late Royal Artillery.
Enquiries, Investigations, Searches.

23, Market Street,
Shepherds Market, W.1.

In 1927 (the same year that their daughter Patricia Fifinella was born) he published *Brighter French* under the name 'H–T–R–.' The book was an immediate success and was reprinted ten times. His *Brighter French Word-Book* followed in 1929, and *Still Brighter French* in 1932.

Prior to the publication of his third book,

H–T–R– and his wife and daughter had moved
to Montpellier in the south of France, where

they lived com-
fortably and happily
throughout the
1930s. At the end
of that decade, the
musically talented
Patricia (pictured
right with him
around 1931, and

below on her *communion solennelle* in May 1939
at Montpellier) was accepted as a student at
the Paris Conservatoire; but then the German

invasion of 1940
changed everything.
Forced 'to get out
with what they
stood up in,' the
family was lucky to
find space on the
last boat leaving for
England. Patricia
later described to
her daughter Anne
'an awful journey'
on a boat overflowing with people. Back in
England (the boat having been held for a time
in Plymouth while a search was made for spies)
they were without money or possessions.

Having returned as virtual refugees, Harry and Marion had serious financial worries for the rest of their lives. They were helped by the then Duke of Bedford (also a Russell, although not known to be related) who gave them accommodation in a house owned by the Bedford Estates—Appletree House at Calstock in Cornwall. They remained there until 1944 when Harry was given the job of head gardener at a property named The Courts at Holt in Wiltshire (which had seven acres of gardens) and they were able to move to its gardener's cottage (above). The property had just been given to the National Trust. A cow was kept as part of the war effort, and there is a record that it was milked by Marion. At some time during the war, they kept hens, but Harry—famously a softie—couldn't bring himself to slaughter them, and this job was left to Marion. From 1946, the family rented a large house at Hilperton near Trowbridge (below) and took in paying guests. H–T–R–'s remarkable linguistic ability  provided some income, and he did translations of German and Italian books (among them, Francesco Perri's *The Unknown Disciple* in 1950). Of the family's situation in those years Anne

Aston writes: 'My grandparents were virtually penniless, but they were very, very happy and I know that my mother (Patricia) adored her father, and it was my mother [pictured here with her parents in 1949] who typed for him in later years when he undertook translations from German to English.'

David Williamson, genealogist at Burke's and Debrett's, developed a close friendship with Patricia. They met in 1945 when both of them (at age 18) started their first job at Geoffrey Bles Publishers. 'We were both very young for our age, very naïve, and very innocent...,' Williamson later wrote to Patricia's daughter Anne. 'We became firm friends, and as you know the friendship endured and I think meant a lot to us both...'

Patricia always described her father, H–T–R–, as the kindest and gentlest of men, and this was David Williamson's memory of him:

> Your grandfather Russell was exactly as one imagines a

H–T–R– AT CALSTOCK

Colonel should be, white-haired, rosy-cheeked,

well-groomed, and with a military bearing. He
was extremely entertaining and witty and I can
remember him sending your mother out of the
room when he was about to tell an only very
slightly improper story (she could tell far worse!)…

Prior to Harry's divorce in 1926, his life and
that of his younger brother Reginald had followed
similar paths. Both were high achievers at school
and both had distinguished military careers. (In
1917 Reginald invented the 'Russell charges'
used by Lawrence of Arabia to destroy railway
lines.) After Harry's divorce, however, the lives
of the two brothers could not have been more
different. Reginald, CVO, CBE, DSO, remained
at the heart of the British establishment. A
military attaché in South America from 1927,
he accompanied the then Prince of Wales on
his tour of the region. In 1931 he was appointed
a member of His Majesty's Bodyguard of the
Honourable Corps of Gentlemen at Arms.

Reginald's daughter, Victoria, married Sir
Mark Baring, who died in 1988. She later
married (in 1997) Major General Lord Michael
Fitzalan-Howard (a brother of the Duke of
Norfolk) who became Marshal of the Diplomatic
Corps and Colonel of the Life Guards (and
held the additional ear-catching title of
Gold Stick in Waiting). His granddaughter
(Harry's grand-niece), Lavinia Gweneth Baring,
was appointed Extra Lady in Waiting to

Diana, Princess of Wales, from 1981 to 1991, and Lady in Waiting from 1991 to 1992.

At the start of 1953, H–T–R– became seriously ill with heart problems, and died in Trowbridge on 30th May of that year. In a heartbreaking letter to Cassells publishers immediately after his death, Patricia wrote of her father's breaking down in distress after his doctor forbade him to continue work on his translation from German of *The Kaiser: a Life of Wilhelm II, last Emperor of Germany* (by Joachim von Kürenberg) and saying 'I must get the book finished, whatever happens.' With the letter, she enclosed Chapter 93 and part of Chapter 94 of his translation.

Not long after H–T–R–'s death, Patricia married a French soldier and lived for a time in Bordeaux. According to Williamson, her parents had been against the marriage but Patricia 'was very determined.' The marriage was unhappy and ended in a divorce less than ten years later.

H–T–R–'s widow, Marion, was in difficult financial circumstances after her husband died. She moved to a flat in Warminster and took a job in a café.

Patricia (with her daughter Anne) also moved to Warminster after her divorce. She took a job in hospital administration, but suffered constant health problems. Her parents had suspected she was affected by TB, but were unable to get this diagnosed. Anne remembers her mother going to her job even when so weak that she was hardly able to do so. Ultimately it was found that Patricia's lungs were scarred with TB.

Through Marion's job at the café, however, life had taken an interesting turn. A patron there was a young career soldier, Drummond Mulberry

(left), whose childhood had not been easy. His mother died when he was a baby; his father—also a soldier—was away on duty for long periods; and Drummond had joined the army as a young teenager. Marion invited him to a family Sunday lunch, and a friendship developed. Drummond bought a house in Warminster, which would be a home for him when he was on leave and in which Marion (later joined by Patricia and

MARION LEE-RUSSELL   PATRICIA RUSSELL-CERET   ANNE CERET-ASTON

Anne) could live for the rest of her life. Today Drummond lives with his wife in Hong Kong, and maintains a close friendship with Marion's granddaughter, Anne, and her family, (all of whom travelled to Hong Kong for a reunion with him at New Year 2010 [*pictured below*]).

All of Harry's children by his first marriage had left Ireland at the time his father's property in Limerick was sold in 1926, three of them moving to Ceylon (Sri Lanka) and one to Brussels. In 1946, however, Harry's eldest son, Richard, 'retired to Bunratty Castle, County Clare'; and in the 1950s, Dunkathel House, a large neo-classical house and estate near Cork City, came into the possession of the Russell family on the death of a cousin, and Harry's son Geoffrey came to live there. The family sold the property in 2003.

Harry's widow Marion died in 1968. His daughter Patricia died in 1979, aged only 52.

Patricia's daughter Anne, a French citizen, remained in Wiltshire. In 1976 she married Brian Aston, and from 1981 to 2005 Anne and Brian (among other careers) took over the running of a post office and shop in Trowbridge previously run by Brian's parents. They have two daughters. Susan (born 1982) holds an MA in Industrial Design & Technology and is a teacher, and Claire (born 1986) is an Accounting & Finance graduate.

DRUMMOND MULBERRY WITH BRIAN, ANNE, SUSAN & CLAIRE ASTON IN HONG KONG

*   *   *

H–T–R– was born into a community of fixed boundaries and values, and of established tracks to be followed: essentially a colonial community. As a decorated soldier in the British Army and a cogent military analyst, he performed with distinction in accordance with the expectations of that community; but his insight into, and sympathy for, the diverse world outside it was apparent in his 1911 essay. He was over fifty when divorce separated him from the life and the financial security into which he was born, and his linguistic and creative abilities then came to the fore. To support his second  family, he produced a series of landmark books, but was happy to take on jobs as unorthodox as private detecting and as physically demanding as gardening when the need arose. In his final years, he experienced financial need, but great family happiness. He left behind a wife and daughter who adored him and a distinctive written legacy, including the most entertaining French language book ever written.

s–j–

DUBLIN, 2010

A MILITARY HISTORY NOTE— In 1900 H–T–R– took
part in the battle at Tugela river, South Africa, and was
'mentioned in Despatches.' The British won the battle,
which was a turning point in the second South African
War and led to the relief of Ladysmith. H–T–R– sketched
the terrain (below) and indicated his own position (left
foreground): 'My battery here X.' On the same day (27th
February) in the first South African War (in 1881) the
British had suffered a major defeat—at Majuba; this is
why H–T–R– used the term 'Majuba day.'

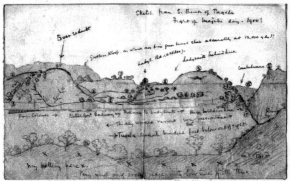

The following are the annotations on his sketch:

Sketch from S. Bank of Tugela. Fight of Majuba day 1900.

Boer redoubt. Grobler's Kloof on which our 6-in gun burst
    shell accurately at 12,000 yards! LadyS[mith] Rd (9 miles).

Kraal. Ladysmith behind here. Umbulwana.

From Colenso – Natal Gov[t] railway – Railway to Ladysmith.

Huge boulders here. Thickly wooded ravine, very precipitous.

Tugela several hundred feet below out of sight. River →.

My battery here X. Very rough and rocky ridge with low
    trees pretty thick.

ERIC FRASER

I F EVER a jacket illustration gave lie to the maxim that one shouldn't judge a book by its cover, it is Eric Fraser's wonderful depiction of the trying-hard dancing girl which appeared on the cover of *Brighter French* in 1927. No

drawing ever has captured more successfully the raw exuberance of the 1920s Paris nightclub, or could better herald the style, gaiety, and 'Gallic salt' of the text. Yet the life of this quiet, hard-working family man, who was one of the most admired and in-demand illustrators of the twentieth century, was far removed from that world. 'There would be no stories of wild nights in Montparnasse or Montmartre,' writes Alec Davis in *The Graphic Work of Eric Fraser*. [1]

Much of Eric Fraser's work is well known, such as his illustrations for the *Radio Times*, his iconic 'Mr Therm' (used for over 30 years by the gas industry), his London Underground railway posters, his stamp designs for the GPO, etc. Unusually for an illustrator, he received much fan mail. He produced book covers and illustrations for the Folio Society and the Limited Editions Club of America, and was always (as in *Brighter*

French) masterful at capturing the essence of the text. An art editor of the *Radio Times*, R.D. Usherwood, said of him:

> …there was never a time when he did not have an uncanny gift for going to the heart of a script and epitomising the whole weight of it in a single drawing. This is essentially an intellectual gift; he draws what he thinks and feels and seems incapable of irrelevance. [2]

Eric Fraser was born in Westminster, in the heart of London, in 1902. His background was not artistic—his father was a solicitor's clerk and his mother was a schoolteacher—but his artistic gifts were recognised early. In 1916, and while still a pupil at Westminster City School, he started attending evening classes at Westminster School of Art. The painter Walter Sickert held life classes at the school, and the 14-year-old Fraser's first attendance at one of these made an unforgettable impression on him:

> I went up with my drawing board to the top floor, entered the life class … and started work. Shortly afterwards, an elderly lady crept up and whispered to me that this was the ladies-only life class, and directed me to the gents-only life class. When I

came home with a drawing of nude ladies, my
parents took a dim view of this and removed
me immediately. So you see Sickert hardly had a
chance to exert an influence on me. [3]

Fraser did return to the evening classes,
however, and in 1919, he won a scholarship
to Goldsmiths School of
Art (part of the University
of London). In 1923, while
still a student, he had an
etching exhibited at the
Royal Academy, and also did
some teaching at the college.
Francis Marriott, headmaster
of Goldsmiths at the time,
later wrote of Fraser:

STUDENT WATERCOLOUR, 1922:
THE ARTIST'S GRANDMOTHER

He was undoubtedly one of the most brilliant
students I had in the School during the 34 years
I was headmaster. [4]

Fraser's most significant magazine client was
the *Radio Times*, but he did work for many
others, including *Vogue*, *Lilliput*, *Pall Mall*,
Nash's Magazine, and did a large amount of
fashion illustration for *Harper's Bazaar* from
1929 to 1937 (before advances in technology
allowed photographs to take over). The
principal purpose of fashion illustration was to
make the clothes look good, and the illustrators
succeeded brilliantly in this (far better than the
photographers who replaced them) not least

because they were unrestricted by the limitations of the human shape. Later Fraser gave his own view of the magazine's house style:

> *Harper's Bazaar* in the thirties—full of magnificent women 10 feet tall, aesthetically unreal, but beautifully created by artists who were also designers—the great era of release from Edwardian Art Nouveau — the new art phœnixed from the ashes of the late war. These women could not be produced through a lens, only we artists could evolve such creatures.
>
> 'Do not fear, the camera will never take the place of the artist,' said the Art Editor, Alan McPeake—forty years on—the artist will never take the place of the camera, I fear. [5]

Using the experience he gained at *Harper's Bazaar*, Fraser would also teach fashion illustration—at the short-lived London branch of the Berlin Reimann School, which closed in 1940.

From 1928 to 1940, Fraser taught at the Camberwell School of Arts and Crafts in London. His subjects included book illustration (his first of 37 book illustration commissions having been for *Brighter French* in 1927). The effect he had on his students is described by William Johnstone, who headed the school from 1938:

> Another splendid teacher was Eric Fraser, the brilliant graphic designer… In all the work he did, whether wood or scraper-board engravings for the *Radio Times*, line drawings or posters, his craftsmanship was superb. He lived his work,

> slept with it, woke with it, taught with it. Fraser was a bulwark in the school, although he was a very gentle, unassuming soul. Fraser would not have fought with a fly, but he was so serious and so expert at what he did that not a student spoke or even sneezed in Eric Fraser's class, they were so fascinated and so impressed by this tiny, frail, blond man. [6]

Sylvia Backemeyer re-quotes these comments of Johnstone in her book *Eric Fraser Designer & Illustrator*, but quickly points out: 'In fact Fraser was nearly six foot tall.' [6]

In World War II, Fraser worked as a Civil Defence Warden. As he later explained, the demands of his civil defence work made it impossible for him to continue teaching at Camberwell:

> One day, exhausted, I went to sleep in the staff room and woke up to find an air raid on, with everyone else in the basement. I gave up teaching after that. [7]

Throughout his career, his style evolved. Alec Davis gives the following assessment of his drawings from the 1920s, many of which are very funny.

> In technique, they showed a reaction against academic representational drawing of the kind which he had turned out steadily and more than competently during his student years. Angles instead of curves, distorted shapes instead of natural shapes—these were the outward and visible signs of an inward and spiritual revolt. They were characteristics that suited the debunking mood of the time ... [8]

After the war, his work would become more serious. He became deeply involved in book illustration, producing remarkable illustrations for the Folio edition of *The Lord of the Rings*, for instance, always adapting his technique to suit the mood of the text. He explained:

> A dramatic story will require an illustration made

up of bold and strongly contrasting masses, while a love story will need a gentle treatment and soft gradations of tone. [9]

Over the decades, his style continued to evolve and, in the words of Wendy  Coates-Smith, in her essay *Eric Fraser the Illustrator*, it became 'tougher and more "graphic"' as the images were competing with other visual material—including television—for space and impact. [10]

Another commentator, however, suggests that the drift from the light and humorous to the serious and more 'graphic' style began as early as 1928, with a commission from the *Radio Times* to illustrate a script that was 'tough and a mite sordid.' The words are those of Rufus Segar who wrote in 1979 in the magazine of the Association of Illustrators:

> … it was the engagement with the text that set him on a serious and dramatic path for illustration. Up to this time he had considered his work light and humorous, the sketches done in simple style, strong line and fractured planning…
> Now the more serious graphic style was founded, the subjects done with more research and

composition, the finishing a steady and inventive application of patient craft. [II]

The most versatile of artists, Fraser also designed panels and stained glass for various churches including St Mary at Hampton (left) and Westminster Abbey, and murals for the Wembley Exhibition of 1923, the 1951 Festival of Britain Exhibition, and the Brussels Exhibition of 1958. His agent throughout his career was R.P. Gossop, a graphic designer who had been head of the design studio at WH Smith.

In 1925, Fraser married Irene Lovett (pictured below with him at the Chelsea Arts Club Ball of that year); and of the couple's close relationship, and of the personality of the artist who was 'so gentle that he would always carefully take a spider outside to set it free rather than kill it,' their son Geoffrey wrote:

He always showed my mother every drawing as it was finished, and before it was sent away. He would leave it on the hall table for her to see, as though, in a way, he felt that it was theirs not his…

He hid himself away too, and only in the later years of his life could he be persuaded very occasionally to appear at functions connected with his work. He never was a speaker. He would be summoned from his studio, when there were visitors to the family home, and he was always pleased to see them. But very soon you would notice that he was no longer present, and he would be found back at his studio desk. I have sometimes wondered whether his prodigious output of drawings was one way in which he defended his shy nature from the world outside. [12]

In 1935, the family settled at Hampton, where Eric Fraser lived and worked (in a studio at the end of the garden) until his death in 1983. The self-portrait opposite was drawn in 1949.

The publishers are extremely grateful to his son the Revd Geoffrey Fraser, and to the Fraser family, for permission to use his sparkling illustrations in this edition of *Brighter French*.

ILLUSTRATIONS

PAGE

The above illustrations were commissioned for the original 1927 edition of *Brighter French* — with the exception of the two marked *, which are additional Fraser illustrations of the period.

[Sources and dates of the drawings included in the foregoing biography of Eric Fraser are on page 291]

FOREWORD [of 1927]
by
H—T—R—

IN THESE HARD DAYS our accomplishments need to be taken seriously. Nobody, for example, plays a violin in public unless he does it extraordinarily well. But nobody *need* play a violin, whereas no one knows when he (or she) may *have to* speak French…with humiliation as the penalty of shortcomings.

In good society, more than ever before, knowledge of French is a tremendous asset, besides being a lasting intellectual joy. A smattering will not do. 'School-French' will not do.

How are the Bright Young People to learn the real French of everyday life? The best way, of course, is by constant intercourse with French-speaking social equals. But this takes time, and Bright Young People are busy.

This little volume aims at filling a gap obvious to all would-be learners. It is mainly a collection of sayings and phrases, some few original but mostly culled from current French literature, avoiding the trite and the stilted, dealing with the spoken language of the dinner-table, the boudoir, the theatre, race-course, promenade-deck, stables, garage, etc. It is believed that even those who know quite a lot of French can read it with advantage. If some of the anecdotes are flavoured with Gallic salt, it is not to be expected that the Bright Young People will complain. Nor yet their Seniors. The volume is not meant for *'la jeune personne,'* but for those who can safely imbibe worldly wisdom together with knowledge of the most subtle of languages.

In the French text, *italics* are used to direct attention to nice points of gender, mood, tense, or agreement. There is no attempt to labour the teaching of syntax, of which a sound understanding is assumed.

The English text must be taken as furnishing 'equivalents' rather than 'translations'; indeed, in many cases wide departures will be found, intended to emphasise the fact that French people naturally *think* quite differently about things, and therefore express themselves differently. The first essential to fluent speech is *to learn to think as a Frenchman thinks.* It will not do to formulate mentally, in English, what one wants to say, and then utter a 'translation.'

That the results of his work may interest and amuse, as well as instruct, is the hope of the Compiler.

H—T—R—

LONDON,
  September 1927

CONTENTS

BRIGHTER
FRENCH

'American in Paris,' pen-and-ink by Eric Fraser,
first published in the BBC *Radio Times* 24 July 1931

PART I

A PRELIMINARY CANTER
Un petit galop

ON LOVE, LIFE, DRINK, CRIME & GAMBLING—
SUR L'AMOUR, LA VIE, L'ALCOOL, LES DÉLITS & LE JEU

A<small>N ATTEMPT</small> to make you *think* as a French person thinks. You can open it anywhere, and learn something.

PROPOS DE TABLE

(ET, AU BESOIN, D'AUTRES MEUBLES)

1. —*De quoi* est-il mort ?
   —On ne sait pas. D'ailleurs on ne savait non plus de quoi il vivait.
2. Ma chérie, écoute, voilà Charlot qui affirme qu'en dansant la vierge a plus de raideur dans la jambe que la femme mariée, et l'épouse fidèle que la femme adultère !
3. Certes, je ne l'ai jamais vue cracher dans les tasses ni se moucher dans les serviettes, mais elle *a bien une tête à le faire*.
4. *Premier soldat—* Le théâtre ne va encore pas trop mal. Ma sœur joue *dans une revue* et elle *se fait* presque *la* solde totale d'un colonel.
   Deuxième soldat— Mais qu'est-ce qu'en dit la femme du colonel ?
5. Il a bien fait une cure à Vichy, mais il paraît qu'il s'obstinait à *couper* cette eau bienfaisante *avec* du whiskey. Ainsi, aucune amélioration, mais au contraire.
6. À New York, chacun porte sous son *frac* une gourde de whiskey.
7. On boit aussi des mixtures frelatées.

TABLE TALK

(SUITABLE ALSO, IF NECESSARY, TO OTHER
ARTICLES OF FURNITURE)

1. —What did he die of?
   —Nobody knows. But then nobody knew what he lived on, either.

2. My dear, just listen, here's Charlie declaring that, in dancing, a virgin is stiffer in the leg than a married woman, and a faithful spouse stiffer than the other sort!

3. True, I've never seen her spit in the cups or blow her nose on the table napkins, but she looks just the kind that would.

4. *First Soldier*— The theatre doesn't do too badly. My sister is playing in a revue just now, and she pockets pretty well all of a colonel's pay.
   Second Soldier— But what does the colonel's wife say about it?

5. He did indeed do a cure at Vichy, but it seems he persisted in mixing the beneficent water with whiskey. So, there was no improvement, but rather the reverse.

6. In New York, everyone carries a whiskey-flask under his evening coat.

7. Also, they drink adulterated mixtures.

8. Lucie *a le pied marin*, mais moi ! Tiens, en cinq jours de traversée j'ai, *pour tout potage*, absorbé une demi-douzaine d'huîtres et *autant de* bouteilles de champagne !

9. Ma cuisinière a *le* nez gros et de la coloration. Elle dit que c'est le fourneau qui *veut* ça !

10. Dans mon petit *patelin* là-bas, j'ai lu cet avis placardé à la mairie :
   — *Tout ivrogne rencontré dans la rue sera passible d'une amende de 10 F. Cette amende sera réduite de 50 pour cent les jours de fêtes légales* et les dimanches.* —
   Après tout, si je suis bien sage toute la semaine, j'ai bien le droit de m'amuser un peu *le* dimanche !

* Les fêtes légales ou *jours fériés* [de 1927] sont : les dimanches ; le 1er janvier ; Pâques et le lundi de Pâques ; l'Ascension ; la Pentecôte (*pron.* pan-kôt) ; le lundi de la Pentecôte ; le 14 juillet (fête nationale) ; l'Assomption (*pron.* a-sonp-si-on) ; *la* Toussaint (1er novembre) ; le 11 novembre (anniversaire de l'armistice de 1918) ; et (*la*) Noël.
[* De nos jours il y a aussi : fête du travail (1er Mai), et armistice de 1945 (le 8 mai).] NOTE— *Le lundi de Pâques*, mais : *le lundi de la Pentecôte.*

11. Cette liqueur *se boit* pure ou *étendue* d'eau.

8. Lucy is a good sailor, but I! Why, for five days of the crossing, all I ate was half-a-dozen oysters and the same number of bottles of champagne!

9. My cook has a big nose and a high colour. She says it is the kitchen range that does it!

10. In my funny little place (village) down there, I read this notice posted at the *mairie* (town-hall): — *Any drunken man found in the street will be liable to a fine of 10 francs. This fine will be reduced by 50 per cent on public holidays* and Sundays.* —
    After all, if I've been good all the week, I've a perfect right to amuse myself a bit on Sunday!

* The *fêtes légales* or *jours fériés* [of 1927 France] are: Sundays; the 1st of January; Easter Day and Easter Monday; Ascension Day; Whit Sunday; Whit Monday; the 14th of July (National Fête); Assumption Day; All Saints' Day; the 11th of November (Anniversary of the Armistice of 1918); and Christmas.
[* Nowadays, also: Labour Day (1st May) and V.E. Day (8th May); (with Whit Monday reinstated in 2008 after its removal in 2005).]

11. This liqueur can be drunk neat or diluted with water.

12. Il a une fâcheuse tendance à *se pocharder*.

13. Ce n'est pas si facile que cela de moraliser un grand pays.

⚜

14. Dans la guerre, la victoire est à celui qui a su *tenir* un quart d'heure *de plus que* l'autre. Dans l'amour, c'est à celui qui a su *tenir à* l'autre un quart d'heure *de moins*.

15. En amour, la suprême habilité *consiste à* faire croire au gibier que c'est lui qui est le chasseur.

16. Un jour qu'il revient il est *tout pantois de* s'apercevoir qu'elle a fort complaisamment accueilli un remplaçant.

17. Elle l'a fait *au vu et au su de* tout le monde.

18. Lui, il restait à Paris. Moi, j'allais, *censément*, retrouver une amie à la plage.

19. *De vous à moi*, l'aimez-vous toujours ?

20. D'abord il m'avait paru intelligent, mais j'arrive à me *rendre compte qu'*il n'est pas très *fin*.

12. He has an annoying propensity for getting tight.

13. It isn't so easy as all that to reform the morals of a great country.

⚜

14. In war, victory is to the fellow who has managed to hold on a quarter of an hour longer than the other. In love, it is to the one who has managed to stick to the other for a quarter of an hour less.

15. In love, the supreme skill lies in making the hunted one believe that he (she) is doing the hunting.

16. He comes back one day and is quite aghast to find she has very calmly taken on another fellow.

    (*Historical present tense*, see pp. 200-203.)

17. She has done it quite openly.

18. As for him, he stayed on in Paris. I went off, ostensibly to rejoin a woman-friend at the seaside.

19. Quite between ourselves, do you still love him (her)?

20. At first he seemed to me intelligent, but I'm coming to realize that he is not very bright.

21. En amour, être raisonnable est avoir tort.

22. —Vous avez bien un amant ?
    —Ça peut vous *faire ?*

23. —Mes affaires de cœur, *c'est mes oignons.* Je ne veux pas que tu t'en occupes.
    —Mais tu en as eu le *béguin* ?

24. Chaque fois que je le vois, il me *raconte des boniments...* qu'il est seul au monde, et *cæte*ra.   [*—ou 'etcétéra' (depuis 1990)**]

25. Ne tardez pas trop ! Vous tourneriez à la *vieille fille !*

26. Mais *que* l'on a peu envie de se marier, lorsqu'on sort de ce théâtre !

27. Les femmes ! À vingt ans, nous leur donnons notre corps ; à trente ans notre cœur ; à quarante ans notre argent ; et à cinquante ans notre nom.

28. Faire de sa femme sa maîtresse, c'est comme *manger* des écrevisses à tous les repas. *Il est des* soupers fins qu'on ne fait bien qu'au restaurant.

29. *Dès qu'*un monsieur est, ou *croit être, souffrant,* il se revêt de sa robe de chambre, et *mande* ses amies chez lui par téléphone.

30. C'est ridicule. Tu sais comme il *s'écoute.*

31. Si je n'*écoutais* que moi-même, *il y a un beau temps que je* l'aurais quitté.

21. In love, to be sensible is to be in the wrong.

22. —Now, have you a lover?
    —Can that matter to you?

23. —My flirtations are my own look out. I don't want you to meddle with them.
    —But you were keen on him?

24. Every time I see him he pitches me the tale…(saying) he's (all) alone in the world, et*cete*ra.   [*1990 *French spelling reform alternative*]

25. Don't delay too long! You might turn into an old maid!

26. But how little one wants to get married, after coming out of this theatre!

27. Women! At the age of 20 we give them our body; at 30 our heart; at 40 our money; and at 50 our name.

28. To make your wife your mistress is like eating crayfish at every meal. There are delicate suppers that are best taken in a restaurant.

29. When a man is ill, or thinks he is, he dons his dressing-gown and summons his lady friends by telephone to come and see him.

30. It's ridiculous. You know how he coddles himself.

31. If I was only considering myself, I'd have left him long ago.

32. Je ne suis plus une gosse à qui *l'*on *fait croire* que les enfants viennent dans les choux !

33. Elle parle comme une *poule* de Montmartre, pour *se donner les gants d'*être affranchie.

34. —Il paraît qu'elle *fréquente* toutes les *sentines* de Londres.
    —Ma foi, oui. Elle est résolue à *faire courte et bonne !*

35. *Dès que* deux êtres se trouvent pour la première fois *en* présence, l'un *prend* nécessairement *le pas sur* l'autre. L'égalité n'existe pas.

36. Je veux *avoir la haute main, pour le cas où* cela tournerait mal.

37. *Moins* une femme se sent digne de respect, *plus* elle en exige.

38. Quand une femme dit trop de mal d'un homme, *c'est qu'*elle est près d'en penser trop de bien.

39. —Je vous demande *pardon*, Mademoiselle, *de* vous déranger.
    —Mais, vous ne me dérangez *nullement*, Monsieur.

40. Voilà une qui *sait vivre !*

⚜

41. Son mari rentra, *aviné* (pris de boisson).

32. I'm no longer a kid (NOTE— *gosse* is masc. or fem.) who can be made to believe that babies are found in cabbage-patches.

33. She talks like a Montmartre tart, to make out she is emancipated.

34. —It seems she is in and out of all the sinks of iniquity in London.
    —Faith, yes. She is determined to have a short life and a merry one.

35. The moment two people come face to face for the first time, one of them of necessity acquires an ascendancy over the other. There is no such thing as equality.

36. I want to keep the upper hand, in case things go wrong.

37. The less worthy of respect a woman feels herself, the more respect she demands.

38. When a woman speaks too badly of a man, it means she is near to thinking too well of him.

39. —I beg your pardon, Mademoiselle, for disturbing you.
    —But you're not disturbing me at all, Monsieur.

40. There's a woman who knows how to do the right thing!

41. Her husband came in, the worse for drink.

42. Je la trouvai là, la figure *assombrie*, un *œil au beurre noir*.

43. *L'on* s'empara de lui et *l'on* le conduisit *au poste*. Note—*Le* poste. (*La* poste : post office.)

44. Le poste de police s'appelle vulgairement *le bloc, la boîte, le quart,* ou *le violon*.

45. Il a déjà fait six mois *de prévention*.

46. On l'a mis en liberté provisoire, *sous caution de* 20 000 francs.

47. Il vient de recevoir une *assignation à comparaître* devant le tribunal.

48. Londres *foisonne en* cambrioleurs et en *montes-en-l'air*. Les *rossignols* et les *pinces monseigneur* sont hors de prix ! À toute sortie de théâtre il y a des *voleurs à la tire*.

49. Il a bien l'air d'un de ces messieurs très dignes, très vénérables, qui finissent *volontiers* en cours d'assises.

50. Il jouait aux courses, mais ce n'est pas *pendable*.

51. C'est *un* cercle *où* l'on joue très fort.

52. C'est bien ma veine ! J'ai pris une *culotte* avant-hier soir au jeu ; une à la Bourse hier après-midi ; aujourd'hui je *joue* un seul cheval et il s'assoit dans l'herbe !

42. I found her there, her face gloomy, (and with) a black eye.

43. They seized on him and led him off to the police station.

44. The police station is vulgarly called the block, the box, the watch, or the fiddle.

45. He has already been in prison (on remand) six months, awaiting trial.

46. He was released on bail, with a recognisance of 20,000 francs.

47. He has just received a summons to appear before the court.

48. London is swarming with house-breakers and cat-burglars. Lock-picks and 'jemmies' are at fabulous prices. At every theatre exit there are pickpockets.

49. He looks very like one of those most worthy and venerable gentlemen that easily end up in an Assize Court.

50. He used to gamble on the race-course, but that's not a hanging matter (not a very dreadful crime).

51. It's a club where they play very high.

52. Just my luck! I took a knock at cards the day before yesterday evening; took another on 'Change yesterday afternoon; today I back one solitary horse, and he goes down!

53. —Un instant, Monsieur… je ne peux pas
    vous recevoir. Je suis en chemise.
    —Prenez tout votre temps, chère amie,
    j'*attendrais que* vous l'*ayez retiré*.

54. Il faut savoir *de quoi parler* dans les dîners.
    Il y a une élégance des *potins* et des
    commérages comme de toutes choses.
    Certaines histoires *passent de mode*.

53. —One moment, Monsieur … I can't see you. I'm in my chemise.
    —Take your time, my dear, I'll wait till you take it off.

54. One must know what to talk about at dinner-parties. There is a stylishness in small-talk and gossip just as in everything else. Some kinds of stories go out of fashion.

PART II

A FEW LITTLE STORIES
Quelques petites histoires

M ANY A Bright Young Person's fortune is made by his (or her) ability to trot out a good story at the right moment. But be sure it is the right moment—and pass on quickly.

POTINS

Surpris au téléphone

Voix nº 1 (*empressée*)— Allô ! Allô ! C'est vous, Germaine ?

Voix nº 2 (*allègre*)— Oui, Monsieur !

Voix nº 1 (*suffisante*)— Bon ! Germaine, vous direz à Madame qu'elle m'attende pour dîner, et que je resterai coucher.

Voix nº 2 (*respectueuse*)— Bien, Monsieur (*insinuante*)... *De la part de qui*, Monsieur ?

La Police privée

Un de mes amis *s'avisa* un jour de *faire pister* la tendre demoiselle qu'il a *mise dans ses meubles*. Il reçut le rapport suivant :

« La dame n'a pas semblé devoir sortir, mais la femme de chambre, suivie, a acheté deux kilos de pêches, qui ne semblaient pas destinées à une seule personne. »

GOSSIP

Overheard on the Telephone

Voice no. 1 (*eagerly*)— Hallo! Hallo! Is that you, Germaine?

Voice no. 2 (*brightly*)— Yes, Monsieur!

Voice no. 1— Right! Germaine, kindly tell Madame to expect me to dinner, and say that I shall be staying the night.

Voice no. 2 (*respectfully*)— Very well, Monsieur …(*insinuatingly*)— What name shall I say, Monsieur? (*Lit.* On behalf of whom?)*

> *De la part de… Very generally used when delivering a message, personally or by telephone etc., for another party. (*Je viens de la part de* — ; *je parle de la part de* —.)

Private Detectives

A friend of mine took it into his head one day to have the loving little lady, that he had provided a flat for, watched. He received the following report:

'The lady does not seem to have had occasion to go out, but her maid, who was followed, bought two kilos of peaches, which would not seem to have been intended for one person only.'

La Plus Belle Lettre d'amour

Voulez-vous que je vous montre *la plus jolie* lettre d'amour que *j'aie* jamais *reçue* ? La voilà— un télégramme—qui dit tout simplement :

Venez —Jeanne.

Le Surnom qui convient

Tout le monde connaît la gentille petite dame qui passe pour avoir tant d'amis parmi les propriétaires de chevaux de course. Elle a, paraît-il, depuis quelques mois, des espérances… On l'a surnommée « l'enceinte des balances ».

The Best Love-letter

Would you like me to show you the nicest love-letter I ever received? Here it is—a telegram—which simply says:

COME —JEANNE.

An Appropriate Appellation

Everybody knows the charming little lady who is reputed to have so many friends amongst the owners of race-horses. It seems that for some months she has been expecting ... She has been named *'l'enceinte des balances.'* ('The weighing-enclosure.')

DÉFINITIONS ET ÉNIGMES

Q.— Qu'est-ce qu'un bon mariage ?
R.— Celui où l'on oublie, le jour qu'on est amants, la nuit qu'on est époux.

Un Bébé.— La conséquence d'une inconséquence.

Le Vice.— Le mal qu'on fait sans plaisir. (—*Colette*)

L'Expérience.— La qualité qui nous permet de ne pas souffrir deux fois de la même façon, du moins avec la même femme.

La Vanité.— L'anse par où les *malins* prennent les *cruches*.

L'Amour.— Opération arithmétique. La preuve faite, on passe à un autre problème.

Un Gentleman.— Celui qui croit à une femme qui lui ment.

Q.— De quoi se passe-t'on mieux à deux que seul ?
R.— Le sommeil.

DEFINITIONS AND RIDDLES

Q.— What is a happy marriage?
A.— One in which they forget during the day that they are lovers, and during the night that they are married people.

A BABY.— The consequence of a slip.

VICE.— Evil done without pleasure.

EXPERIENCE.— The quality which enables us not to suffer twice over in the same way, at any rate not with the same woman.

VANITY.— The handle by which clever folk hold stupid people. (*Cruche, lit.* jug, jar.)

LOVE.— An arithmetical operation. The proof once established, one passes on to another problem.

A GENTLEMAN.— One who believes a woman who is telling him lies.

Q.— What is it that one can do without, two by two, better than alone?
A.— Sleep.

Chez le grand couturier—At the Couture House

PART III

A LITTLE TRIP TO PARIS
La Passade à Paris

MERELY AN EXCUSE for introducing you to a few more 'words' ... the powder being, so to speak, concealed in something like jam.

LA PASSADE À PARIS

PREMIER ACTE

*Le 21 avril 1927. Chez Lui. Fumoir d'un joli
cagibi à Mayfair. 22 h. 30. Luxe discret,
rien de superflu. Grands fauteuils en cuir.
Divan. Coussins. Un bon feu répand une
illumination suffisante. Gramophone. Cigare.
Cigarette.*

ELLE (*grave, après avoir arrêté Galli-Curci en
pleine course*).— Mon ami, le moment est venu
de penser aux choses sérieuses.

LUI (*inquiet*).— Mais à quoi, donc ? Tu n'es
pas par hasard…

ELLE (*ferme*).— Je n'ai plus rien à me
mettre !

LUI (*soulagé*).— Ah-h !

ELLE (*toujours ferme*).— Je redis. Voilà mai
qui s'abat sur nous—et je n'ai plus rien à me
mettre !

LUI (*sceptique mais indulgent, comme il
sied*).— À d'autres ! *Je te vois venir* avec cette
histoire-là ! Alors, ça c'est Paris, hein ?

ELLE (*extasiée*).— Tu l'as dit, chéri ! Nous
partirons après-demain. Le temps de me
concilier la famille… qui devient encombrante
comme toujours à cette saison… de régler mon
passeport…

A LITTLE TRIP TO PARIS

ACT I

*21st April, 1927. The smoking-room of a jolly little
nook in Mayfair. Time 10.30 p.m. A discreet
luxury, with nothing superfluous about it.
Big leather armchairs. A divan. Cushions. A
nice fire provides sufficient illumination. A
gramophone. A cigar. A cigarette.*

SHE (*solemnly, having checked Galli-Curci in
full career*).— My dear, the time has come to
think of serious matters.

HE (*uneasily*).— Why, think of what? You
aren't by chance...

SHE (*firmly*).— I haven't a rag to my back!

HE (*relieved*).— Ah-h!

SHE (*still firmly*).— I repeat. Here is May
coming on us—and I haven't a rag to my
back!

HE (*sceptical, but suitably indulgent*).— Tell
that to the Marines! I can see through you and
your tale! So, it's Paris, I suppose?

SHE (*delightedly*).— You've said it, darling!
We'll start the day after to-morrow. Just time
enough to make my peace with the family, which
is becoming a nuisance as it always does at this
time of year...and to fix up my passport...

Lui (*surpris*).— Ton passeport ! Mais qu'est-ce-qu'il peut avoir, ton passeport ?

Elle.— Certes, il est toujours bon,... mais il faut y renouveler la photographie...

Lui.— ? ? ? ?

Elle.— Tu crois que je vais *trimbaler* ce misérable petit chapeau de l'année dernière, même en photo ?

Lui.— Mais non, naturellement !

Elle (*rêveuse*).— Paris, mon chéri, Paris en avril, c'est délicieux !

DEUXIÈME ACTE

Le 22 avril 1927. Gare de Victoria. Bureau de renseignements au premier. 11 h. 30. Il entre. L'employé, qui le reconnaît, s'empresse.

L'emp.— Bonjour, monsieur ! Il y a longtemps que vous n'avez favorisé nôtre pauvre « Southern »... Vous voulez, n'est-ce pas, deux billets de première, aller et retour, pour Paris, *via* Folkestone-Boulogne ? Quand *comptez-vous* partir ?

Lui.— On a vraiment tort de calomnier le « Southern » ! Datez les billets pour demain. Je prendrai... nous prendrons... le train de 14 h.

L'emp.— C'est ça. Et vous retenez deux places dans le pullman ?

He (*surprised*).— Your passport? What can be wrong with your passport?

She.— It's still valid, of course…but I must renew the photograph…

He.— ? ? ? ?

She.— Do you suppose I'm going to cart around that miserable little last year's hat, even in a photo?

He.— Oh! no! of course not!

She (*dreamily*).— Paris, my darling, Paris in April. Delightful!

ACT II

22ⁿᵈ April, 1927. Victoria Station. Information Bureau on 1ˢᵗ floor. Time 11.30 a.m. HE enters. The clerk, who recognizes him, is all attention.

Clerk.— Good morning, sir! It's a long time since you patronized our poor 'Southern'… You want, of course, two first-class returns to Paris, *via* Folkestone-Boulogne? When do you think of travelling?

He.— It's really very wrong of people to run down the 'Southern.' Date the tickets for tomorrow; I'm going by…we're going by…the 2.00 p.m.

Clerk.— Quite so. And you will book two seats in the Pullman?

Lui.— Je préférerais la petite case au fond du wagon, si elle est libre... Elle l'est ? Bon... Faites voir le plan... Bon... *Marquez-moi*—marquez-nous—pour les 22 et 23, côté fenêtre... le 23, vous savez, c'est pour moi—pour nous—le nombre fortuné...

L'emp.— Je l'espère bien, monsieur. Vous avez toutes les chances d'être les seuls occupants. J'ai remarqué que dans les trains de Paris, on n'arrive jamais à louer les quatre places de la « case »... à moins qu'on ne les loue toutes à la fois à quelque partie carrée, à quelque fournée d'amis... au point de vue de la compagnie, c'est assez sérieux... c'est tout, monsieur ?

Lui.— Oui. Non. Sur le bateau, retenez-moi une cabine sur le pont, par le travers... Comment ! c'est drôle, ça ! elle aussi est numérotée 23 !... et les places dans le pullman à Boulogne... et... Dame ! j'oubliais cette petite Louise ! et un billet de deuxième pour Louise... pour la bonne de ma femme, vous savez ? Nous réglerons les suppléments au besoin...

L'emp.— Parfaitement, monsieur ! (*Travaux de calcul.*) C'est £18 exactement, monsieur.

Lui (*en aparté*).— Tonnerre de bonsoir de sac à papier !

L'emp.— *Paris, monsieur, Paris en avril, c'est délicieux !*

He.— I'd rather have the little compartment at the end of the car, if it's free…It is? Good…Let's see the plan of the car…Right…Book me—book us—seats 22 and 23, on the window side…23 you know is my—is our—lucky number…

Clerk.— I'm sure I hope so, sir. You have every chance of being the only occupants. I've noticed that on the Paris trains we never manage to let all four seats of that compartment, unless we let them all together to some party of four or some group of friends…from the Company's point of view it's rather a serious thing. And is that all, sir?

He.— Yes. No. On the boat, reserve me a deck cabin, amidships…what's that…that's funny…its number is 23 too!…and book seats in the Pullman at Boulogne…and Good Lord! I was forgetting all about Louise! and a second-class ticket for Louise…my wife's maid, you know? We'll pay any extras where necessary…

Clerk.— Precisely, sir. (*Makes calculations.*) That will be exactly £18, sir.

He.— (*Quite untranslatable. Must be taken as a cry from the heart of one who realizes that eighteen pounds IS eighteen pounds, and that this is only a beginning.*)

Clerk.— *You know, sir, Paris in April, delightful!*

TROISIÈME ACTE

Le 23 avril, 1927. Gare de Victoria. Quai de départ. 13 h. 50. Cohue normale. Défilé à la barrière sous l'œil froid du « flic » qui guette les mauvais sujets. On pense forcément aux écarts les plus innocents de sa jeunesse. LUI et ELLE vont s'installer aux 22 et 23.

ELLE.— Le seul secret de voyager en confort, c'est de ne pas *s'empêtrer* de colis !

LUI.— Je dirais plutôt que c'est d'en empêtrer Louise ! À propos, où est-elle ? Elle parlementait avec John…

ELLE.— À coup sûr il lui faisait un sermon au sujet de sa bonne conduite dans une capitale païenne… tout en lui rappelant ses préférences en fait de photos artistiques… mais la voilà !…

LUI.— Je vais *arrimer* ça dans le filet, bien en vue… votre nécessaire et tout…

ELLE.— Louise, asseyez-vous là au 24, en attendant le départ. Cela *écartera* les couples venus par hasard…

(En effet, il arrive deux couples retardataires, l'un grossier, l'autre industriellement fastueux. Tous les deux se retirent, découragés, vers le salon. Coup de sifflet. Doucement, le train s'ébranle. Louise *s'esquive* dans les deuxièmes.

ACT III

*23rd April, 1927. Victoria Station. Departure Platform.
Time 1.50 p.m. The usual crowd. The procession
through the barrier under the cold eye of the
'tec' who is on the look-out for the 'bad hats.'
One can't help thinking of the most harmless
escapades of one's youth. HE and SHE proceed
to install themselves in numbers 22 and 23.*

SHE.— The one secret of travelling in comfort is not to load oneself up with packages!

HE.— I should have said it was to load 'em up on Louise! By-the-by, where is she? She was palavering with John...

SHE.— It's a sure thing he was giving her a sermon on her behaviour in a pagan capital... whilst reminding her of his preferences in the way of artistic photographs...but here she is!...

HE.— I'll stow these things in the net, your dressing-case and all, well in sight...

SHE.— Louise, sit there on number 24 until we start, that will keep away any chance couples...

> (As a matter of fact, two late-coming couples do turn up, one vulgar, the other industrially pompous. Both retreat, disheartened, towards the body of the car. The whistle sounds. The train moves out gently. Louise slips away to the seconds.

Dans le couloir, un accent américain chante « *Ma chérie, Paris, en avril, c'est délicieux ! »*)

QUATRIÈME ACTE

Le 23 avril, 1927. La jetée à Folkestone. 15 h. 45. La foule s'achemine vers le paquebot. « All passports ready, please ! Have your passports ready ! » Le monsieur à la coupée inspecte les billets, livre les cartons de débarquement aux passagers. Les grues tapageuses font décrire des trajectoires einsteiniennes aux gros fardeaux qu'elles déposent dans les soutes. Trois coups de sirène assourdissants. On lâche les amarres. On commence à relever la passerelle. Au dernier moment, surgit la femme fatale, corpulente, couperosée, chargée d'innombrables paquets en papier gris, qui est restée là sur la jetée, inconsciente. Elle se précipite sur la passerelle qui déjà tient à peine. Un marin flegmatique la recueille. Elle en est quitte pour la perte de quelques paquets, qui flottent tristement dans l'eau huileuse, et qu'elle ne semble point regretter. Le bateau glisse le long du quai, sort du port, gagne le large. Les passagers sont accoudés aux bastingages.

In the corridor, an American accent sing-songs '*My darling, Paris, in April, delightful!*')

ACT IV

23rd April, 1927. The quay at Folkestone. Time 3.45 p.m. The crowd is wending its way towards the boat. 'All passports ready, please! Have your passports ready!' The gentleman at the gangway inspects the tickets, issues the disembarkation cards to the passengers. Clattering cranes cause their heavy burdens to describe Einsteinian curves as they deposit them in the holds. Three deafening blasts on the siren. The hawsers are cast off. They begin to clear away the gangway. At the last moment, there appears the inevitable woman, stout, red-faced, laden with innumerable brown-paper parcels, who has remained behind on the quay, oblivious to everything. She rushes on to the gangway, now barely touching. A phlegmatic sailorman gathers her. She gets out of it with the loss of a few parcels, which are floating sadly in the oily water, and which she does not seem to regret at all. The boat glides along the quay, clears the port, heads out to sea. The passengers are leaning over the rails.

(NOTE— A traveller by sea is '*un passager.*' A traveller by land is '*un voyageur.*')

Lui.— Voilà, chérie, je viens de te dénicher une chaise.

Elle.— Merci, mon ami. Tu seras assez aimable pour chercher Louise et lui demander ma couverture de voyage et mon coussin.

Lui (*de retour*).— Tu n'as aperçu personne *de notre connaissance* à bord ?

Elle.— Si. Ce vieux *raseur* de P— et *sa moitié*… mais ils sont rentrés dans l'escalier. Et toi ?

Lui.— La petite D—. Elle est seule, en apparence.

Elle.— Elle sait sauver les apparences ! Elle est fine, cette gosse. Elle m'a dit, une fois, qu'elle ne savait seulement pas ce que c'était que l'amour, qu'elle ne le connaissait que par ouï-dire ! Après tout, c'est une façon de prononcer « Hughie-dear » !…

Lui.— Il commence à faire frais. Si tu rentrais à la cabine ? La mer aussi devient houleuse. Mais tu as le pied marin ! Tu n'as pas besoin de remèdes.

Elle.— Mon cher, on naît avec où sans le mal de mer. La victime, si elle veut s'en préserver, n'a qu'à rester sur *le plancher des vaches !* Il n'existe pas d'autre remède. Maintenant, je vais me reposer. Garde-toi de *braconner* dans la chasse de « Hughie-dear »…

Lui.— Sois tranquille ! En qualité d'avocat, il m'est arrivé d'effleurer en quelque sorte la loi.

He.— There, darling, I've just found you a chair.

She.— Thanks, my dear. Now will you be so kind as to find Louise and ask her for my travelling-rug and cushion?

He (*returning*).— You haven't seen anyone we know on board?

She.— Yes. That old bore of a P— and his better half…but they have gone below again. Have you seen anyone?

He.— The little D— woman. She is by herself, or so it appears.

She.— She knows how to save appearances! She is pretty cute, that kid. She told me once she didn't even know what love meant, that she only knew about it from hearsay (*par ouï-dire*). That's one way, after all, of pronouncing 'Hughie-dear'!

He.— It's turning chilly. Suppose you went back to the cabin? The sea is turning lumpy, too (*developing a swell*). But you've got your sea-legs! You don't want remedies.

She.— My dear man, one is born with or without sea-sickness. A victim to it, if he wants to escape it, had better stay on dry land (*terra firma*)! There is no other remedy. Now, I'm going to lie down. Mind you don't poach on Hughie-dear's preserves…

He.— You may be easy! In my capacity of barrister, it has been my fate to skim the law a

Aussi, me souviens-je que *braconner*, c'est *chasser* (et par extension, *pêcher*) en des endroits réservés : *primo*, en des temps défendus ; *secundo*, avec des engins prohibés ; *tertio*, sans permis ; et je t'assure que je n'ai pas la moindre disposition pour porter atteinte à ce bon Hughie sous aucun des trois rapports !

ELLE.— Va-t-en ! vaurien. Tu es impayable !

    (Deux nouveaux mariés,* en lune de miel, passent devant le hublot de la cabine. Affectueusement penché sur sa compagne l'époux heureux murmure—*Et Paris, mon chou, en avril, c'est délicieux !*)

* See p. 240

CINQUIÈME ACTE

Le 23 avril 1927.—17 h. 20.—Boulogne. Le bateau est entré dans la passe à vitesse réduite. Une belle arrivée. Le couchant promet. Les stewards emportent les valises et encombrent les couloirs. Les passagers vont former des groupes près de la coupée. Les doyens affirment que le port sent mieux qu'au temps jadis. Les jeunes écoutent, déférents mais sceptiques.

LUI.— Holà, porteur, holà !... Mais regarde un peu, lui aussi c'est le numéro 23 !... Voilà, on se retrouvera à la douane... Viens, chérie, attention à la passerelle... c'est plutôt raide et peut-être glissant... accroche-toi à la *main courante*...

bit. So I remember that to *poach* is to *chase* or to *hunt* (and by extension, to *fish*) [NOTE.—*Pêcher*, to fish; *pécher*, to sin] in preserved places, *firstly*— at forbidden times; *secondly*—with prohibited engines; *thirdly*—without leave; and I assure you I'm not in the least inclined to offend against poor dear Hughie in any one of the three ways!

SHE.— Get away with you, you worthless creature! You are too priceless!

(Two newly-married folk, on their honeymoon, pass the porthole of the cabin. Leaning affectionately over his companion, the happy young husband murmurs, *Paris, my pet, in April, delightful!*)

ACT V

23rd April, 1927.—5.20 p.m. Boulogne. The boat has entered the harbour-channel at reduced speed. It is a pleasing end to the journey. The setting sun holds good promise. The stewards are carrying up the suitcases and blocking the passages. The passengers form into groups by the gangway. The old hands have it that the port smells better than in times past. The young ones listen, deferential but sceptical.

HE.— Hi! Porter, hi!... Why, just look, he is number 23, too!... There, we'll meet at the Customs... Come, darling, mind the gangway, it's pretty steep and may be slippery...hang on to the hand-rail...

(On piétine les corridors du vaste hangar. On exécute marches et contremarches. L'agent de la Sûreté, bienveillant, timbre les fiches des passeports. Les formalités de la douane s'imposent.)

ELLE.— Pourvu qu'on n'exige pas que *j'étale* le contenu de mes malles !

LE DOUANIER.— Madame, vous n'avez rien à déclarer ? Pas de parfums, de cigarettes, de... ? ? ?

ELLE.— Non, monsieur, rien, ... ab-sol-u-ment, rien !

LE DOU.— Et vous, monsieur, vous n'avez rien à déclarer ?

LUI.— Si, monsieur, j'ai une demi-livre de tabac anglais, une boîte de cigarettes turques (à moitié vidée), deux boîtes d'allumettes de provenance finlandaise, un flacon de bay-rhum américain,...

LE DOU.— Ça suffit, monsieur, et amplement ... je mets l'hiéroglyphe sur votre petite société des nations, et je vous souhaite bon voyage !

LOUISE.— Madame ; madame ! Que madame regarde seulement là-bas ! Le grand Africain qui s'est fait pincer ! Il paraît que c'est un *trafiquant de coco* qu'on a recherché pendant des mois ! On me disait ça sur le bateau... Le voilà *fait aux pattes !*

LUI.— Louise ! Vous songez toujours au

(They tramp the corridors of the huge shed. They execute marches and countermarches. The agent of the *Sûrête*, a friendly fellow, stamps the pages of the passports. The Customs formalities have to be gone through.)

SHE.— If only they don't insist on my spreading out all I have in my trunks!

THE CUSTOMS OFFICER.— Anything to declare, madame? Any scents, cigarettes, any... ???

SHE.— No, monsieur, nothing, ab-so-lute-ly nothing!

THE CUSTOMS OFFICER.— And you, sir, have you anything?

HE.— Yes! I've a half-pound of English tobacco; a half-empty box of Turkish cigarettes; two boxes of matches of Finnish origin; a bottle of American bay-rum...

THE CUSTOMS OFFICER.— That, sir, is enough, quite enough... I will append the hieroglyphic to your little League of Nations and wish you a happy trip!

LOUISE.— Madame, madame! Will madame just look over there! The big African who's been arrested! It seems he is a cocaine trafficker they've been looking for—for months past! They were telling me about it on the boat!... There he is, nicely handcuffed!

HE.— Louise! You're always thinking of the

cinéma ! C'est tout simplement un pauvre —
de musicien qui a *égaré* son trousseau de clefs,
de sorte qu'il ne peut pas ouvrir l'étui de son
saxophone ! Tenez ! empoignez le nécessaire de
Madame, et en voiture !

 (On s'installe dans le compartiment. On
lit. On sommeille. Les paysages fuient à
toute vitesse. Le bruit monotone des roues
chante—*À Paris ! À Paris !*—en avril—*c'est
dé-li-ci-eux !*... *c'est dé-li-ci-eux.*)

SIXIÈME ACTE

*Le 23 avril 1927.—Paris.—Le rapide de Boulogne
a ralenti en atteignant la grande banlieue
où les voies de triage enchevêtrent leurs rails.
Les pylônes de signaux poussent partout. Les
voyageurs troquent leurs casquettes contre
des chapeaux mous, melons, ou autres. Les
voyageuses sortent les houppettes pour fignoler
leurs toilettes. À 21 h. 05 le train s'arrête au
quai d'arrivée de la Gare du Nord avec un
retard de 10 minutes seulement. Pas si mal.
Des porteurs nombreux affluent. On descend.*

Lui (*au porteur*).— Nous prenons deux
taxis... l'un pour madame et moi, l'autre
pour la femme de chambre. Nous emportons
seulement ces deux valises et le nécessaire de
madame et nous filons devant... *arrangez-vous*
avec mademoiselle pour le reste... Tenez ! voilà

cinema! It's only a poor — of a musician who has mislaid his bunch of keys and can't open the case of his saxophone! Here, take hold of madame's dressing-case, and off with you into the train.

(They take their places in the compartment. They read. They snooze. The countryside flies by at full speed. The monotonous sound of the wheels sings—*To Paris! To Paris! ... in April; de-light-ful ... de-lightful!*)

ACT VI

23rd April, 1927.—Paris.—The fast train from Boulogne has slowed up on reaching the outer suburbs where the sidings form a tangle of rails. Signal posts start up everywhere. The male travellers change their caps for soft hats, bowlers, or what-not. The ladies get out their powder-puffs and touch themselves up. At 9.5 p.m. the train draws up on the arrival platform of the Gare du Nord, only ten minutes behind time. Not at all bad. Many porters swarm round. The people get out.

HE (*to the porter*).— We'll have two taxis ... one for madame and myself, the other for the maid. We'll take with us only these two suitcases and madame's dressing-case, and we'll go on ahead ... you'll fix up with mademoiselle for the other things ... Here! Take the

les bulletins... il y a quatre malles à *repêcher*...
et voilà vingt francs de pourboire...

LE PORT.— Ben m'sieur... en-ten-du m'sieur
... m'sieur n'a que s'en rapporter à moi... j'y
veillerai...

ELLE.— Louise, *est-ce là tout ?* Vous n'avez
rien oublié ? Tâchez de vous amener à l'hôtel
le plus tôt possible...

LUI (*au chauffeur*).— À l'hôtel Soleil, rue de
la Madone, 75 ! On peut gazer !

(Démarrage sensationnel... course
fougueuse... quelques petits *engueulements*
de rien de tout... arrêt brusque devant la
porte de l'hôtel... On est arrivé !)

ELLE (*pratique*).— Et tout ça pour 3 F 50 !

LUI.— *Ça te change de Londres, hein ?* En
effet, au prix que coûtent les taxis à Londres
un Rothschild est *capable d'y regarder à deux
fois !*

(Débarquement définitif. Salutations
empressées du « manager » accueillant,
du concierge, enfin de la totalité du
personnel. Petite cérémonie de rédaction
des renseignements de la fiche policière...
Ascenseur... Réédition momentanée de la
pose *Enfin seuls !*... Louise... Les malles...
L'eau, bonne et chaude, coule bruyamment
en coulisse... Inutile d'insister. On est de
trop.)

baggage-checks…there are four trunks to fish out…and here's 20 francs for you. (tip)…

THE PORTER.— Right, sir! I understand, sir! You may leave it to me, sir, I'll see to it…

SHE.— Louise, is that all now? You've not forgotten anything? Try to get along to the hotel as soon as possible.

HE (*to the chauffeur*).— Hôtel Soleil, 75 rue de la Madone, and you can step on the gas!

> (A sensational start… a headlong career… some little scatterings of abuse that don't amount to anything… a sudden stop at the hotel door… Here we are!)

SHE (*practically-minded*).— And all that for 3 francs 50!

HE.— A change from London, isn't it? What with the cost of taxis in London, a Rothschild might look twice at 'em!

> (A final disembarkation. Assiduous greetings from the welcoming manager, from the concierge, in fact from all the staff. A little ceremony to be gone through in filling up the registration form… The lift… A hurried reproduction of the '*Enfin Seuls*' stunt… Louise arrives…and the trunks… Nice hot water burbles noisily off-stage… No need to go on… One is *de trop*.)

23 h. 00.—ELLE (*assoupie*).— Vraiment, mon chéri, à Paris, en avril, c'est délicieux !

23 h. 15.—LOUISE (*assoupie, elle aussi. Elle a dû flanquer une gifle à un valet de chambre trop entreprenant*).— C'est rigolo. Je ne sais pas ce que j'ai, mais il faut toujours que les hommes me *pelotent*, et tout de suite !

CHEZ LE GRAND COUTURIER

ELLE.— Mon ami, voudriez-vous m'accompagner chez mon couturier ?... Non, non, rassurez-vous... pas d'essayage aujourd'hui ! Mais peut-être ça vous amuserait de *jaser*, en regardant défiler les mannequins ?

LUI.—Volontiers, chère madame, *à condition que* vous m'accompagniez *plus tard* chez mon tailleur.

(TAXI-AUTO. PLACE VENDÔME. ASCENSEUR.)
ELLE.— On dit que *la taille remonte* cette année.

LUI.— Qu'elle remonte ou qu'elle *baisse*, il importe de *remonter le* garde-robe !

ELLE.— C'est la *coupe*, vous savez, qui signale une robe *de prix*.

LUI.— Si bien que celle-là doit valoir au moins le triple de son *pesant d'or !*

ELLE.— Pour les robes d'après-midi surtout rien qui soit *trop habillé*. Cela *fait province*.

11.00 p.m. SHE (*half-asleep*).— Really, darling, in Paris, in April, it's delightful!

11.15 p.m. LOUISE (*also half-asleep. She has had to smack the face of a too enterprising valet*).— It's a funny thing. I don't know what's wrong with me, but all the men must start messing me about, and straight away too!

AT THE COUTURE HOUSE

SHE.— *Mon ami*, would you care to come with me to my dressmaker's? ... No, no, don't be afraid...no trying-on today! But perhaps it would amuse you to have a chat and look at the mannequins parading?

HE.— Gladly, dear lady, on condition that you come with me to my tailor's afterwards.

(TAXI-CAB. PLACE VENDÔME. LIFT.)

SHE.— They say waists are going to be higher this year.

HE.— Whether they go up or down, the wardrobe has to be replenished!

SHE.— It's the cut, you know, that marks the costly dress.

HE.— So that that one there must be worth at least three times its weight in gold!

SHE.—For afternoon frocks especially, one must not have anything too 'dressy.' That looks provincial.

Lui.— Les décrets de la province sont insondables !

Elle.— Depuis déjà *pas mal de temps* on ne *décolore* plus les cheveux.

Lui.— Mais les femmes ont besoin de *truquer* quelque chose… *aussi*, maintenant, *décolorent-elles* leurs fourrures !

Lui.— Qui est donc cette jolie femme là-bas, celle qui est *tout de blanc vêtue*, avec une toque blanche et slave ?

Elle.— Mon cher, je ne saurais vous dire. Elle a le goût qui retarde !

Lui.— Je ne suis pas de votre avis, madame !

Elle.— Mais, mon cher, sans un certain *ensemble* de nuances assorties il n'y a pas d'élégance possible ! L'harmonie d'abord, et à tout prix !

Lui.— Mais l'harmonisation est difficile ?

Elle.— *Pas tant que cela*. On nous *en* a vraiment *gavé*, *du blanc*, cet hiver.

Lui (*entre ses dents*).— Je la trouve ravissante, la petite *ourse* blanche ! Si qu'on pourrait seulement…

Elle.— Tiens ! Cette jeune fille à gauche… je reconnais cette robe. Elle est de chez Poisson Sœurs… *Il n'y a qu'elles* pour *s'obstiner dans* les volants froncés !

Lui.— Des *poissons volants*, évidemment !

Elle.— Voilà dix minutes que vous *zyeutez* ce petit mannequin ! Elle vous plaît ? *Un vrai*

HE.— The decrees of the provinces are inscrutable! (*Les décrets de la Providence sont insondables.*)

SHE.— For quite a long time now people haven't been dyeing their hair.

HE.— But women must fake something, so now they're dyeing their furs!

HE.— Who's that pretty woman over there, the one all in white, with a white Russian kind of toque?

SHE.— My dear, I couldn't tell you. Her taste (in clothes) is out-of-date!

HE.— I do not agree with you, madame!

SHE.— But, my dear man, there can be no possible elegance without some kind of harmony of suitable shades. Harmony first and at any price!

HE.— Getting the harmony is difficult, I suppose?

SHE.— Not so difficult as all that. We've really been overdone with white this winter.

HE (*to himself*).— I think she's ripping, the little white lady-bear! If one could only...

SHE.— Hallo! That young girl there on the left... I recognize that dress. That's from Poisson Sœurs... Trust them to stick to gathered flounces!

HE.— Flying Fish, evidently!

SHE.— You've been eyeing that little manne-quin for the last ten minutes! You like her? A

numéro, n'est-ce pas ? Mais, mon pauvre ami, *vous vous abusez*. Je la connais. Les apparences *nonobstantes*, elle est mère de famille, et *travailleuse*, et *avec ça* d'une probité déconcertante...

LUI.— Madame, je tiens de Marcel Pays qu'il ne faut croire à la vertu des femmes qu'à la dernière extrémité... *encore* doit-on *l'imputer à* sa malchance ou à sa maladresse !

ELLE.— Mais il a dit aussi que deux agrafes et quatre épingles suffisent à défendre une vertu solide, et elle doit en avoir plus que ça...

LUI.— *Il n'est de* vertu solide que défendue par l'amour... mais entretenez-moi des souliers, *je vous en prie !*

ELLE.— Les souliers ! Ils *se démodent* tous les mois ! Le goût change à chaque instant, quant à la *forme*, plus ou moins ronde, ou carrée... ou pointue... la longueur de *l'empeigne* (*pron.* an-pè-ne)... le nombre et la disposition des *barrettes*, *l'échancrure*, la *garniture*, et les *nuances*.

Pour *accompagner* les robes dans les tons clairs il faut des souliers de *daim* ou de *chevreau* beige très clair ou gris perle... avec les bas *assortis*, ai-je besoin de *le* dire ?

Avec les tons sur *fond* noir, les souliers seront uniquement noirs, avec les bas *taupe*...

LUI.— *Tope là !*

real topper, isn't she? But, my poor friend, you are quite mistaken. I know her. Appearances notwithstanding, she is the mother of a family and hard-working, and over and above that bafflingly moral...

HE.— Madame, I've learnt from Marcel Pays that one should never believe in the virtue of women save in the last extremity...and even then one should put it down to one's own bad luck or clumsiness.

SHE.— But he has also said that two hooks-and-eyes and four pins are enough to defend a real virtue, and she must have more than that...

HE.— The only real virtue is one defended by love...but I beg you, discourse to me about shoes!

SHE.— Shoes! They go out of fashion every month! Taste changes every instant, as regards shape, more or less rounded, or square, or pointed...the length of the toe-cap, the number and arrangement of the straps, the (size of the) opening, the ornamentation, and the tints.

To go with dresses of light tone you must have shoes of buckskin or beige kid, very light-coloured or pearly grey...with stockings to match, need I say?

With tones on a dark foundation, shoes must be black and nothing else, with *taupe* (mole-coloured) stockings...

HE.— I quite agree! I'm with you there.

ELLE.— Avec les robes blanches, ou presque, les souliers seront blancs, non sans un petit *rappel de couleur*, si toutefois *il s'agit* d'une toilette habillée…

LUI.— Et pour les *villégiatures*, comment transporter tout ça ?

ELLE.— Dans les chapeaux, la mode *chôme*. Mais le petit chapeau de feutre est un peu abandonné pour le chapeau de paille, *ni* grand *ni* petit.

LUI.— Je suis encore aux souliers. Avec les costumes tailleurs, les souliers *en lézard* sont très chic, n'est-ce pas ?

ELLE.— Mais oui, et *par-dessus le marché*, ils ne *se lézardent* jamais ! Quant à la pelleterie, les fourrures sont *hors de prix* cette année ! Les *zibelines*, les *chinchillas*, les *visons*, les *martres*, tout ça n'est qu'*un* rêve. Revenons à nos lapins ! … Mais regardez donc la baronne ! Voilà une que la *baisse* du franc *n'indispose* pas trop !

LUI.— Son mari n'est pas jaloux ?

ELLE.— On ne sait pas. La jalousie, vous savez, n'a aucun chic. Si vous êtes jaloux, si vous en mourez, faut tâcher qu'on n'en voie rien. Ça fait à la fois *vieillot* et *du dernier bourgeois !*

LUI.— Ce que vous dites là me rappelle un mot d'une de mes amies qui discutait la colère. —La colère, insista-t-elle, est assez gentille comme sentiment de matin. Peut se porter avec le costume

SHE.— With white, or nearly white, frocks, shoes must be white, not without a little reminder of colour, especially if it be a case of a 'dressy' toilette …

HE.— And when you go paying visits in the country, how do you carry all these things about?

SHE.— In hats, the fashion is at a standstill. But the little felt hat is being rather forsaken for the straw hat, not very big and not very small.

HE.— I'm still thinking of the shoes. With tailor-mades, the lizard-skin shoes are very smart, don't you think?

SHE.— Yes I do, and moreover they don't ever crack! As for the furriery, furs are extravagantly dear this year! Sables and chinchillas and American martens and the other sort of martens, all these are only a dream. Back to our rabbits! … But just look at the Baroness! There's someone who isn't much worried over the fall of the franc!

HE.— Her husband isn't jealous, is he?

SHE.— Nobody knows. Jealousy, you see, is not at all smart. If you're jealous, if you're dying of jealousy, you must try not to let anyone see anything. That would seem awfully elderly and horribly middle-class!

HE.— What you're saying now reminds me of a saying of one of my women-friends who was holding forth on bad temper. A bad temper, she maintained, was quite all right as a morning sentiment. One could wear a bad temper with

tailleur, ou bien encore *dans l'intimité, en pyjama...* mais impossible, ignoble même, avec la robe d'après-midi ou la toilette du soir !

ELLE.— Après tout, elle est peut-être *dans le vrai !* Mais où est donc mon sac ? Il me semble que j'ai une *tache de suie* sur le nez !

(ASCENSEUR. PLACE VENDÔME. TAXI-AUTO.)

CHEZ LE TAILLEUR DE MONSIEUR

(*Ayant bel et bien fouillé la collection, Madame a fait son choix. Jusque-là, Monsieur n'y est pour rien.*)

LUI.— Un *complet* dans cette étoffe, c'est combien ?

TAILL.— C'est douze cents francs, Monsieur ... avec le change et tout Monsieur sait bien que...

LUI.— Ça va. Je prends un complet. *Pour quand* l'essayage ?

TAILL.— *D'ici trois jours*, Monsieur. Ça sera pour mercredi, à onze heures n'est-ce pas ?

LUI.— Bon !

ELLE.— Je suis *bien aise* d'avoir déniché pour vous quelque chose de nouveau. Comme vous êtes *moutonniers, vous autres* hommes ! Sans nous, vous ne songez jamais *à rien changer !* Maintenant, allons goûter au Ritz !

a tailor-made, or still better in strict privacy, with pyjamas…but it was quite impossible, and even outrageous, with an afternoon frock or an evening dress!

SHE.— After all, perhaps she is right! But where's my bag? It looks to me as if I had a smut on my nose.

(LIFT. PLACE VENDÔME. TAXI-CAB.)

AT MONSIEUR'S TAILOR

(*Having very thoroughly rummaged over the display of patterns, Madame has made her choice. Up to this Monsieur hasn't counted.*)

HE.—How much for a suit of that stuff?

TAILOR.— That would be 1,200 francs, monsieur…what with the exchange and everything monsieur knows that…

HE.— That'll do. I'll have a suit. When shall I try on?

TAILOR.— In three days' time, monsieur. That will be on Wednesday, shall we say at 11 o'clock?

HE.— Right!

SHE.— I'm very glad I've ferreted out something new for you. How sheeplike you men are! If it wasn't for us you'd never dream of changing anything at all! Now, let us go and tea at the Ritz.

TÉLÉPHONE

(*Lui et Elle visitent Charles, au Ritz-Palace.*)

Elle.— Chéri, cours au téléphone et *appelle-moi* Susie *à l'appareil.*

Lui.— Charles, vous permettez que je *donne un coup de téléphone ?*

C.— Faites !

(Lui court au téléphone, *décroche*, passe le *récepteur* à l'oreille.)

Lui.— Allô ! Mademoiselle, allô ! *La ville*, s'il vous plaît.

—Allô ! La ville ? Donnez-moi s'il vous plaît Trudaine 08 75 (Trudaine zéro-huit soixante-quinze).

—Allô ! C'est toi, Susie ? … Peste ! Il y a une *dérivation !* Quelqu'un sur la ligne ! Retirez-vous, imbécile !
(Le signal « pas libre » résonne. Lui *raccroche*.)

—Allô ! C'est toi, Susie ? C'est Jean qui parle… C'est que… J'ai eu du mal à t'avoir…
(*Une friture épouvantable…*)

(*Voix de la demoiselle de l'hôtel.*— Vous avez eu votre communication ?)

THE TELEPHONE

(*SHE and HE are calling on CHARLES, at the Ritz.*)

SHE.— Darling, run to the 'phone and get Susie (on) for me.

HE.— Charles, may I use your 'phone?

C.— Go ahead!

(He runs to the 'phone, unhooks, puts the receiver to his ear.)

—Hallo! Mademoiselle, hallo! Give me the (public) exchange, please.

—Hallo! Exchange? Give me, please, Trudaine 08 75.

—Hallo! That you, Susie?... Oh! blast! The line's crossed. Someone on the line! Get off, you idiot!

(The 'engaged' signal sounds. 'HE' hangs up the receiver.)

—Hallo! That you, Susie? Jean speaking... It's... I've had some trouble to get you...

(*A terrible crackling noise...*)

(*Voice of the girl at the Hotel Exchange.*— Have you had them?)

(*Voix de la demoiselle de la ville.*— On ne r-r-r-r-répond pas !)

Lui.— *Ne coupez pas*, Mademoiselle, ne coupez pas !

(Silence.)

AU TÉLÉPHONE

The English rules of the game demand that in spelling out (*en épelant—pron. é-plan*) a word, one should say:

A *for* Alfred.

B *for* Benjamin.   *Etc.*

In French one says:

A *comme* Antoine.

B *comme* Babette.   *Etc.*

Also—in French [*1927 usage*]—one indicates numbers somewhat as follows:

(7) Sept—quatre et trois.

(8) Huit—deux fois quatre.

   Etc.

2010 NOTE— En anglais, on donne les numéros de téléphone chiffre par chiffre, par ex. 020- 7973 1992 : '*oh two oh, seven nine seven three, one double nine two.*' (Pour le chiffre 'o', on dit '*oh*' ou '*zero*').

(*Voice of the girl at the Public Exchange.*—Sorry—there—is—no—r-r-r-eply!)

He.— Don't cut me off, mademoiselle … don't cut me off!

(Silence.)

TELEPHONING

In calling from a hotel, or an office with a Private Branch Exchange, it is usual to ask the operator (*téléphoniste*) there for '*la ville*'—meaning the public exchange (*le central*). The operator at the *central* answers '*j'écoute*' ('I am listening'), whereupon the caller proceeds as above to give the Exchange and number required.

2010 NOTE— Currently, telephone numbers in English-speaking countries tend to be written in groups of three or four (or five) and spoken in single digits, while in France they are written in pairs (with spaces between) and are spoken in French as double digits, e.g. 01 40 63 38 00 : « *zéro-un, quarante, soixante-trois, trente-huit, zéro-zéro* ».

Ses parents tiennent à le faire médecin.
—His parents want him to be a doctor.

[Autobiographical pen-and-ink by Eric Fraser,
first published in *Commercial Art* magazine, 1926]

PART IV

TWO WONDERFUL VERBS
Deux verbes merveilleux

FAIRE & PORTER

Here we revert to the task of trying to make you think like a Frenchman. The two simple verbs *Faire* and *Porter*, with their innumerable applications, are veritable key-words. Have at them, then! But don't try to absorb it *all* at one sitting, or you may get mental indigestion. We offer you 210 specimens illustrating *Faire*, with 30-odd for *Porter*... and probably some have still eluded us!

FAIRE

1. Il fait son droit à Paris.

2. Il a suffisamment de loisir pour faire les armes.

3. Elle se pique de faire la cuisine.

4. C'est une étourdie, qui n'a jamais tenté de faire aucun métier.

5. Il a la prétention de se faire notaire.

6. Ses parents tiennent à le faire médecin.

7. Ils font les *gens de lettres*.

8. Il fait l'amant chez elle.

9. Il se fait plus fort qu'il ne l'est.

10. Elle fait la malade.

11. Elle s'en est tirée en faisant la morte.

12. Elle fit mine de ne pas comprendre.

13. Il fait semblant de ne pas ouïr.

14. Il fait la sourde oreille à nos plaintes.

FAIRE

1. He is studying law in Paris.

2. He has enough spare time to go in for fencing.

3. She prides herself on doing the cooking.

4. She is a giddy sort of person, who has never tried to follow any trade.

5. He is ambitious to become a notary.

6. His parents want him to be a doctor (want to make him a doctor).

7. They set themselves up as literary people (writers).

8. He plays the lover at her place.

9. He makes out he is stronger than he is.

10. She is shamming ill.

11. She got out of it by pretending to be dead.

12. She pretended not to understand.

13. He pretends he cannot hear.

14. He turns a deaf ear to our reproaches.

15. Elle fait toutes mes délices.

16. Je l'aurais acheté, mais le bouquiniste l'a fait cent francs.

17. Pendant une heure il faisait les cent pas devant sa porte.

18. Ne trouves-tu pas que le gris fait bien avec le bleu dans son boudoir ?

19. J'ai à faire la revue de toute cette paperasse. (NOTE— To review troops, etc., is *passer en revue*.)

20. Pour réussir cela, il faudrait faire un miracle.

21. Et avec cela, il a le toupet de faire le généreux envers elle.

22. L'embarcation commença à faire eau.

23. Il faisait nuit, mais il faisait beau temps.

24. Les bandits ont fait main basse sur les voyageurs.

25. Je vous conseille de ne jamais lui faire une confidence.

26. Mais, mon ami, vous me faites la morale. Je n'y tiens plus !

27. Ne faites pas la moue !

28. Comment cela se fait-il ?

29. Elle lui fit entendre qu'elle avait l'intention de partir le lendemain.

15. She is everything to me.

16. I'd have bought it, but the bookseller wanted 100 F for it.

17. For an hour he did sentry-go before her door.

18. Don't you think the grey goes well with the blue in her boudoir?

19. I have to go through all these (useless) papers.

20. To bring that off, one would have to work a miracle.

21. And, moreover, he has the cheek to make out he is generous to her.

22. The boat began to leak.

23. It was dark, but it was fine (weather).

24. The bandits seized the travellers.

25. I advise you never to trust him/her with a secret.

26. But, my friend, you are lecturing me. I won't have any more of it!

27. Don't be grumpy!

28. How does that come about?

29. She gave him to understand that she meant to leave the following day.

30. Quelle idée vous faites-vous de ce récit extraordinaire ?
31. Faites-moi savoir de vos nouvelles dès votre arrivée là-bas.
32. C'est un homme à tout faire.

33. Elle a visité tous les bureaux de placement, à la recherche d'une bonne à tout faire.
34. Elle est à tout faire.

35. Je n'ai rien à faire cet après-midi.

36. Je n'ai que faire d'elle.

37. Il faisait haut le pied.

38. Il a tout fait à la fourche.

39. Ici la route de Bayonne fait fourche.

40. Il se fait honneur de la connaître.

41. Elle fait admirablement les honneurs de l'ambassade.
42. Je lui fais l'honneur de l'avoir reconnu le premier.
43. C'est un homme qui a toujours fait honneur à ses promesses.
44. Malheureusement j'ai à faire honneur à une grosse échéance.

30. What do you think of this extraordinary story?
31. Let me hear from you as soon as you get down there.
32. He is a jack-of-all-trades.

33. She's been to all the agencies (registry offices), seeking a general servant.
34. She is fit for (ready for) anything.

35. I've nothing to do this afternoon.

36. I don't want to have anything to do with her.
37. He vanished (made off).

38. He's done it all anyhow (carelessly).

39. Here the Bayonne road branches off.

40. He is proud to know her.

41. She does the honours admirably at the Embassy.
42. I give him the credit of having been the first to see it.
43. He's a man who has always fulfilled his promises.
44. Unluckily I have to meet a big bill.

45. Il lui a fait réparation d'honneur.

46. Voulez-vous me faire l'honneur de venir avec moi ?

47. Voila la bonne qui vient faire la chambre.

48. Elle fera aussi le linge et le lit.

49. Ce maudit chien ne fait qu'aboyer.

50. Il a fait son chemin.

51. Nous ferons Noël à Paris.

52. Il s'est fait connaître.

53. Les jeunes ménages de nos jours ne veulent pas faire d'enfants.

54. Évidemment, c'est à faire.

55. Cela fera tout aussi bien votre affaire.

56. Laissez-moi faire !

57. Le gamin lui fit un pied de nez et disparut.

58. Elle fait du bien, elle fait l'aumône.

59. C'en est fait !

45. He has made him an ample apology.

46. Will you do me the honour of coming with me?

47. Here's the maid come to clean (tidy up) the room.

48. She will also get the washing ready and make the bed.

49. That accursed dog never stops barking.

50. He has got on (done well for himself).

51. We shall spend (celebrate) Christmas in Paris.

52. He has distinguished himself (come to the front).

53. The young married couples of our day don't want to have any children.

54. Evidently it's got to be done.

55. That will do you just as well.

56. Leave it to me!

57. The urchin cocked a snook at him and disappeared.

58. She does good, she gives alms.

59. That's finished it (that ends it)!

60. Les vendanges sont faites.

61. Il lui a porté bonheur, elle en fait vendange.

62. Les vins de cette année ne sont rien de merveilleux, mais ils se feront.

63. Elle m'en a fait l'aveu.

64. Laissez-moi tranquille, vous me faites mal !

65. Il a fait volte-face.

66. Il a tout essayé, mais rien n'y faisait.

67. Ces montagnards sont faits (rompus) à la fatigue.

68. Comme c'est exaspérant, ce bruit du trafic !

69. Ah ! Je m'y suis fait.

70. Cela me fait pitié.

71. C'est à faire pitié !

72. Il vaut mieux faire envie que pitié.

73. Avant de partir en voyage autour du monde elle fait maison nette.

74. Il fait des folies pour cette jeune femme.

60. That business is over and done with (*lit.* the gathering of the grapes is finished).
61. He has brought her good luck, she is making the most of it.
62. The wines of this year are nothing wonderful, but they will improve.
63. She has confessed it to me.

64. Leave me alone, you're hurting me!

65. He has whipped round (turned about).

66. He has tried everything, but nothing would do (suit).
67. These mountain people are inured to fatigue.
68. How exasperating this noise of traffic is!

69. Ah! I'm used to it.

70. That excites my compassion.

71. It's lamentable!

72. Better be envied than pitied.

73. Before starting off on her voyage round the world she is dismissing all her servants.
74. He is rashly extravagant over this young woman.

75. Il a fait la noce de son temps.

76. Cela a fait son temps.

77. C'est justement cela qui fait faute.

78. Il vient de me faire un mauvais coup (tour).

79. Demain nous ferons *le* tour *du* lac.

80. Venez faire *un* tour *de* jardin.

81. Ce petit bibelot est fait de main de maître.

82. Elle l'a fait en un tour de main.

83. À qui à faire ?

84. Faites qu'elle soit contente.

85. J'aurai fort à faire pour la persuader.

86. Vous me donnez fort à faire pour débrouiller ce complot.

87. Je ferai tout mon possible.

88. Je fais de mon mieux.

89. Sept et cinq font douze.

75. He has led a riotous life in his day.

76. That has served its time (is out of date).

77. That is just what is lacking.

78. He has just done me a dirty trick.

79. To-morrow we'll go for the trip round the lake.

80. Come and take a turn round the garden.

81. This little trinket is a masterpiece.

82. She has done it in a twinkling.

83. Whose deal is it (cards)?

84. See that she is satisfied.

85. I shall have a stiff job to persuade her.

86. You are giving me a lot of trouble over unravelling this plot.

87. I shall do my very utmost.

88. I'm doing my best.

89. Seven and five are (make) twelve.

90. Combien font cinq fois cinq ?

91. Je vous fais grâce de tout ça.

92. Cette démarche de son gouvernement *fait honte à* Son Excellence [*nom féminin*].

93. Elle [*i.e. Son Excellence—n.f.*] leur *fait honte de* cette ingratitude.

94. En effet, ça m'a fait plaisir.

95. Cela m'a fait *du* bien.

96. Qu'est-ce que ça fait ? Ça ne fait rien !

97. Faisons table rase de ces préjugés.

98. Elle y fait trop de façons.

99. Elle vient de me faire une scène.

100. C'était sa fête, aussi avons-nous fait un extra.

101. Elle faisait (défaisait) ses malles.

102. Comme il fait bon ici !

103. Il fait des dépenses fantasques.

104. Ne me parlez pas des vêtements tout faits ! —Je n'achète que les vêtements faits sur mesure.

90. What is five times five?

91. I forgive you all that.

92. This step (taken by) his Government makes his Excellency ashamed.
93. He reproaches them for this piece of ingratitude. (See p.276)
94. Indeed, it pleased me.

95. That has done me some good.

96. What does that matter? It matters nothing!
97. Let us put aside (wipe the slate clean of) these prejudices.
98. She makes too much fuss about it.

99. She has just made a violent attack upon me.
100. 'Twas her birthday, so we went a bit of a splash.
101. She was packing (unpacking) her trunks.

102. How comfortable it is here!

103. He is spending money wildly.

104. Don't talk to me about ready-made clothes! —I only buy clothes made to measure.

105. Je fais pour le colonel, qui est absent.

106. Mais, mon cher, tu en fais une tête !

107. La batterie a fait quelques kilomètres au trot.

108. Que veux-tu que j'y fasse ?

109. Faites entrer le suivant !

110. Faites venir le garde-chasse.

111. Pour gagner, il faut faire cent points.

112. Faites voir !

113. Faites savoir à Monsieur Picot que je l'attends.

114. Il fait bonne chère.

115. Il est dévot, il fait maigre les vendredis.

116. J'en fais peu de cas.

117. Il fait grand cas de cette affaire.

118. Il ne fait cas que de ses placements.

119. Le patron fit voile pour Douvres.

105. I'm acting for the Colonel, who is away.

106. My dear chap, how glum you look about it!

107. The battery covered several kilometres at a trot.

108. What do you suppose I can do about it (how can I help it)?

109. Show the next one in!

110. Send for the gamekeeper.

111. To win, you must score 100 points.

112. Show (it to) me!

113. Tell Monsieur Picot that I am waiting for him.

114. He lives well (does himself well).

115. He is devout, he fasts (abstains from meat) on Fridays.

116. I'm not worrying about it.

117. He thinks a lot (puts a high value on) this business.

118. All he cares about is his investments.

119. The skipper set sail for Dover.

120. Je ferai cause commune avec toi dans cette affaire.
121. Enfin, ça fera encore l'été.

122. Ça ne te fait rien, n'est-ce pas, qu'ils dînent avec nous ?
123. Alors, c'est décidé. Vous ne nous faites pas faux bond ?
124. Il fait ces calculs de tête.

125. Il n'est jamais trop tard pour bien faire.

126. Là ! Voilà une bonne chose de faite !

127. Et grand bien vous fasse !

128. Ils ont profité de cette occasion inattendue pour faire fortune.
129. Les paysans sont à faire la moisson.

130. On l'a fait périr dans le désert.

Note the use of FAIRE *to dispense with the Passive Mood, so often avoided when possible. Thus:*

131. Il a fait sa soumission, mais le roi *l'a fait pendre.*
132. Les deux frères *se firent tuer* dans cette attaque.
133. S'il ne s'en donne garde, il *se fera rouler.*

120. I'll make common cause with you in this business.
121. It will last out the summer, anyhow.

122. You won't mind, will you, if they dine with us?
123. So, that's settled. You won't fail us (let us down)?
124. He does these calculations in his head.

125. Never too late to mend.

126. There! That's well over!

127. And much good may it do you!

128. They took advantage of this unexpected opportunity to enrich themselves.
129. The peasants are busy with the harvesting.

130. They gave out that he perished in the desert.

Passive Mood:

131. He made his submission, but the King had him hanged.
132. Both the brothers got killed in this attack.
133. If he doesn't watch it, he'll be done down (swindled).

134. Elle n'en veut faire qu'à sa tête.

135. Elle ne fait que d'arriver.
     (This expresses a yet more recent arrival than *elle vient d'arriver*.)

136. Il se fait tard.

137. Reste donc ! Je te fais peur ?

138. Si l'on faisait du sentiment en affaires on n'en finirait pas.

139. Elle a fait exprès de ne pas le saluer.

140. Il est assez difficile de lui faire la conversation.

141. Elle est là, et il faudra faire avec.

142. Elle en a fait une demeure charmante.

143. Il tient à lui faire justice.

144. Il tient à faire justice de cette dame.

145. Je me fais une raison.

146. Et comment que tu feras ?*
     * Thoroughly ungrammatical, of course... but an uneducated person might very well say it! And he might say it to *you*!

147. Ah ! ça m'y fait penser !

134. She will only do just what she pleases.

135. She has only just this moment arrived.

136. It's getting late.

137. Now, stay! Do I frighten you?

138. If you indulged in sentiment in business there would be no end to it.

139. She made a special point of not bowing to him.

140. It's rather difficult to carry on a conversation with him (her).

141. She's here, and we'll have to put up with her.

142. She has turned it into a charming abode.

143. He wants to right his (her) wrongs.

144. He wants to treat this lady according to her deserts.

145. I'm taking the law into my own hands (am going to put a stop to it).

146. And how are you going to manage it?

147. Ah! That reminds me!

148. Deux minutes avant le coup de sifflet, il arrive à la gare, avec ses sœurs, qui *lui font la conduite*.

149. Il a fait la vie de son temps.

150. Il ne fit pas de frais pour me séduire.

151. Il est certain que nous ne ferons rien pour nous voir.

152. Je suis bien aise d'en avoir fait mes frais.

153. Vous ne voyez pas qu'elle vous fait marcher ?

154. Il plante ses dents dans des idées *toutes* faites, et on n'arrive pas à *les lui faire* lâcher.

155. Parmi l'assistance on ne remarqua que très peu de *gens faits*.

156. Avez-vous déniché quelque chose de neuf en fait* de cocktails ?

157. Vous pouvez tenir cela pour fait.

158. Cela vaut fait.

159. C'est déjà un grand pas de fait.

160. Au fait*, tu as raison.

161. Il me racontait ses hauts faits* là-bas.

   * This is of course a substantive (or adverbial locution), not the *p.p.* of the verb [156, 160, 161].

148. Two minutes before the whistle sounded, he arrived at the station, with his sisters, who were looking after him.

149. He has led a riotous life in his day.

150. He made no effort to please me.

151. It's quite certain we shan't try to meet.

152. I'm glad to be out of it without a loss.

153. Don't you see she is humbugging you?

154. He sticks his teeth into these ready-made notions, and one cannot make him let them go.

155. Amongst those present one noticed only very few grown-up people.

156. Have you unearthed anything new in the way of cocktails?

157. You may consider it already done.

158. It's as good as done.

159. That goes a long way towards it.

160. After all (all things considered), you're right.

161. He was telling me about his exploits over there.

162. Il *n'y a pas de quoi* être très fier, tout compte fait.

163. Elle fait la belle, ce soir.

164. Sur la terrasse du château un paon (*pron.* pan) faisait la roue (se pavanait).

165. Je ne m'en fais pas.

166. Il *fait beau voir* qu'il est venu.

167. Il *ferait beau voir* qu'il est venu le premier.

168. Voilà une heure que vous me faites faire le pied de grue.

169. Encore une fois qu'elle fait une gaffe.

170. Monsieur et Madame Un Tel nous prient de faire part de la naissance de leur fille : Françoise.

171. Je sais déjà. Justement je viens de recevoir le (billet de ; la lettre de) faire-part.

172. Pige donc comment il fait sa tête !

173. Non, mais la tête que fera monsieur en apprenant cela !

174. Je n'ai pu me faire une opinion précise *sur* cette nouvelle.

175. Si nous faisions dodo ?

162. There's nothing to be very proud of, when all's said and done.
163. She is showing herself off this evening.

164. On the terrace of the castle a peacock was spreading his tail.
165. I cannot do without it.

166. It is good to see that he has come.

167. It would be odd (strange) to find that he was the first to come.
168. You've kept me waiting (*lit.* standing on one leg like a crane) an hour.
169. Once more she has put her foot in it (said, or done, the wrong thing).
170. Mr. and Mrs. So-and-so request us to announce the birth of their daughter: Françoise.
171. I know. I've just received the formal (letter of) announcement.
172. Just look at the airs he gives himself!

173. Goodness! What will the master say when he finds that out!
174. I haven't been able to come to any exact conclusion (to form any definite opinion) about this news.
175. Suppose we went to sleep (now)?

176. Les munitions vinrent rapidement à faire défaut.
177. Il faisait l'intérim de son chef.

178. Le docteur X— fera l'intérim du docteur Y— pendant les vacances.
179. En Irlande, la pluie fait l'intérim des averses.
180. Le chat faisait ses ongles sur le bord du divan.
181. L'ambassadeur fit l'éloge des aviateurs français.
182. Mon cher, quel faste ! Auriez-vous fait un héritage ?
    [*Note use of conditional mood to express doubt.*]
183. Elle voulait faire une vie digne d'elle.

184. Marie donna un brusque coup de barre. Elle faisait fausse route.

185. Nous ferons route ensemble.

186. —Et demain ?
    —Demain il fera jour !

187. Je fais fi de ses manigances.

188. Je ne fais qu'une passade à Dinard.

189. Attendez! Le temps de me faire faire la barbe!

176. Ammunition soon ran out (was exhausted).

177. He was deputising for his chief.

178. Dr X— will act as *locum tenens* for Dr Y— during the holidays.

179. In Ireland, it rains when there are no showers.

180. The cat was sharpening its claws on the edge of the divan.

181. The Ambassador *spoke in praise* of the French aviators.

182. My dear fellow, what magnificence! Have you come into a legacy?

183. She wanted to lead a life worthy of herself.

184. Marie changed the subject abruptly (*lit.* put the tiller hard over). She was on the wrong tack (making a blunder).

185. We'll go together.

186. —And (what about) to-morrow?
     —Tomorrow 'twill be daylight!
     ('Sufficient unto the day is the evil thereof.')

187. I despise his tricks.

188. I'm only making a short stay in Dinard.

189. Wait! Just a moment till I get a shave!

190. Vous ne vous faites plus la barbe à vous ?

191. Il réussit à se faire jour à travers la foule.

192. Allez, bombez la poitrine, bombez ! Faites beau !

193. Deux bataillons des Grenadiers *faisaient la haie* de Victoria à Hyde Park Corner.

194. Tiens ! Je vais faire ma *réussite*.

195. Il se fit connaître, en déclinant son nom et qualités.

196. Elle a trop fait la *bombe*.

197. Voulez-vous que je vous la fasse connaître?

198. Voilà la « troisième » qui va encore faire ses *frasques* !

199. Une jolie fille me faisait vis-à-vis dans le Métro.

200. La pauvre petite *se faisait une fête* de venir.

201. Il faisait un somme après le déjeuner.

202. Il ne fait que des coq-à-l'âne (*invar.*)

203. À mon âge, mon ami, je ne me vois pas faisant le soleil !

190. Don't you shave yourself now?

191. He managed to make a way through the crowd.

192. Come now, throw out your chest! Show yourself off!

193. Two battalions of the Grenadiers were lining the streets from Victoria to Hyde Park Corner.

194. Well! I'm going to tell my fortune (by the cards).

195. He introduced himself, reciting his name and titles.

196. She has led too much of a hectic life.

197. Would you like me to introduce her to you?

198. There's the third-floor woman off again on her larks!

199. A pretty girl was sitting opposite me in the Underground.

200. The poor little girl was looking forward to coming.

201. He was having a nap after luncheon.

202. He's only talking rot!

203. At my age, my friend, I don't see myself doing 'grand circles' (on the horizontal bar—gymnastics).

204. En natation je fais des progrès. J'en suis maintenant à faire la planche !

205. Il faut faire patte de velours dans cette affaire.

206. Son voisin de table lui faisait du pied, du genou, du coude. Il s'évertuait à forcer son attention.

207. Voilà ! Le plus fort est fait !

208. Il a fait son portrait en pied.

209. En vous le prêtant, j'en avais fait mon deuil.

210. NOTE—
« Fis-je » ; « Fit-il » ; « Fit-elle ».

204. In swimming, I'm making progress. I've got as far as floating now!
205. We'll have to go very cautiously ('pussyfoot') in this business.
206. The man sitting next her was touching her with his foot and his knee, and nudging her with his elbow. He was trying hard to force her attention.
207. There now! The worst is over!

208. He has done (painted) a full-length portrait of her (him).
209. When I lent it to you I said good-bye to it (had finished mourning for it, *i.e.* never expected to get it back).
210. NOTE— *The narrative construction, meaning:* 'I (he, she) remarked (said).'

PORTER

1. Le conférencier *porta* l'attention de l'assistance *sur* le modèle qu'il exposait.
2. Elle porte le deuil *de* sa mère.

3. Portez vos regards de ce côté.

4. Dès sa jeunesse elle portait au vice.

5. Ne crois pas trop que la vertu porte sa récompense en soi.
6. Ce placement porte 6 pour cent.

7. Cela pourrait bien vous porter préjudice.

8. Il a porté la main sur sa femme.

9. Là, c'est la femme qui porte la culotte.

10. Les discours de cet individu pouvaient porter la foule à faire des excès.
11. Quelques-uns se sont portés à des voies de fait.
12. C'est l'orateur qui doit en porter la peine.

13. Les chats noirs me portent malheur.

14. C'est le maire qui portera la parole.

PORTER

1. The lecturer drew the attention of his audience to the model he was exhibiting.
2. She is in mourning for her mother.

3. Cast your eyes this way.

4. From her youth she was inclined to be vicious.
5. Don't be too ready to believe that virtue carries its own reward.
6. This investment pays 6 per cent.

7. That might very well prejudice you (damage you).
8. He struck his wife.

9. In that menage, the grey mare is the better horse ('tis the wife that wears the breeches).
10. The speeches of this person might have excited the mob to commit excesses.
11. Some of them did indulge in acts of violence.
12. The speaker is the man that ought to suffer for it.
13. Black cats bring me ill-luck.

14. The Mayor will speak (for all of them).

15. Mesdames, messieurs, portons un toast à la réussite de cette entreprise !

16. —Vous porterez, n'est-ce pas, ce bon Dupont à l'élection ?

17. —Est-ce qu'il se porte candidat ?

18. Jamais de la vie je n'y ai porté mes pas !

19. Il buvait sec, mais il savait porter son vin.

20. Ce pistolet porte à mille mètres.

21. Au bord de la mer, c'est très bien porté de sortir sans chapeau.

22. Elle porte depuis trois mois.

23. Sur quoi porte votre plainte ?

24. Ce vin est fort. Il porte à la tête. Il porterait bien de l'eau.

25. La célèbre tour de Pise porte à faux.

26. Son yacht (*pron.* i-ak) porte bien sa toile.

27. Le vaisseau, à sec, portait au sud-ouest.

28. La déclaration qu'il a faite ne porte rien de tout cela.

29. Elle portera volontiers témoignage.

30. Elle me porte sur les nerfs.

15. Ladies and gentlemen, let us drink to the success of this undertaking!
16. —You'll vote, won't you, for old Dupont, at the election?
17. —Is he standing (is he a candidate)?

18. I've never been near the place in my life!

19. He drank hard, but he knew how to carry his liquor.
20. This pistol carries 1000 metres.

21. At the seaside, it is quite good style to go about without a hat.
22. She is three months gone (in the family way).
23. What is it you complain of?

24. This wine is strong. It goes to the head. It would stand diluting quite well.
25. The celebrated tower of Pisa leans over.

26. His yacht carries her canvas well.

27. The ship, under bare poles, was heading south-west.
28. The declaration he has made expresses nothing of the kind.
29. She will gladly give evidence (bear witness).

30. She gets on my nerves (irritates me).

NOTE ALSO THE FOLLOWING:

À bout portant.	Point-blank.
L'un portant l'autre.	On an average.
Être bien (ou mal) portant.	To be fit (well), or unfit (ill).
Se porter bien (ou mal).	

All the compound nouns made up of '*porte-*' (*e.g. porte-cigarette*) are MASCULINE in gender, whether written with a hyphen or not. The majority of these are INVARIABLE*, but in such as do change in the plural (usually those written without a hyphen, *e.g. portefeuille*) the '*porte-*' portion is of course INVARIABLE.

Un porte-cigaret*te*	A cigarette *holder* [*—1920s parlance, also: fume-cigarette*].
Un porte-cigaret*tes* *	A cigarette *case*.

[*2010 NOTE: The above usage remains correct, however the 1990 French spelling reform allows an option of variable plurals for ~60 previously invariable '*porte-*' words]

PART V

USEFUL TIPS
Le Mot juste

HERE ARE a few miscellaneous 'tips' which you will find useful for giving your French a little extra polish.

USEFUL TIPS
Le Mot juste

'WHEN'

When is rendered by either Quand or Lorsque.

Quand may be either an adverb or a conjunction ; Lorsque is a conjunction simply. As conjunctions, they are to all intents and purposes interchangeable.

When? as an interrogative adverb of time, must be rendered by Quand followed by verb in the indicative. *Thus:*

> Quand sera-t-elle de retour ?
> When will she be back?

When, equivalent to 'whereas', is rendered by Quand followed by verb in either indicative or conditional. *Thus:*

Vous vous plaignez, quand vous *avez*
  tout lieu de vous montrer content.
You complain when you have every
  reason to show you are pleased.

Vous parlez, quand vous *devriez* vous
  taire.
You talk when you ought to keep
  silence.

Quand, meaning 'even if', is often followed
by 'Même' (or more rarely by 'Bien même'), in
which case the following verb must be in the
conditional:

Quand même ça serait, elle a dû
  s'abstenir.
Even if it were so, she should have
  kept away.

The final 'e' of Lorsque is elided only before
—il, elle, on, en, un, une:

On s'amuse lorsqu'on est jeune.
One has a good time whilst one is
  young.

'MORE'

MORE, used absolutely, is rendered by DAVANTAGE—which may also mean 'longer' (in time). DAVANTAGE is peculiar in that it must always stand at the end of its clause. *Thus:*

> Il a de l'argent, mais il en veut
>   davantage.
> He has money, but he wants more.

> Vous seriez mal avisé d'y rester
>   davantage.
> You'd be ill-advised to stay there
>   any longer.

But it would be correct to say « *J'ai fait plus* » [I've done more (than that)] when this remark immediately follows and refers to something said by someone else.

MORE, meaning 'MORE THAN,' is PLUS QUE...
    Thus: Elle a voyagé plus que lui.

(—but if a number follows, it is PLUS DE):
    Il y retournait plus de dix fois.

Meaning 'MORE OF' it is PLUS DE... *Thus:*
    Elle a donc plus d'expérience que lui.

THE MORE…THE MORE… is PLUS… PLUS…
Thus:

> Plus on fréquente chez lui, plus on
> l'apprécie.
> The more one sees of him, the more
> one appreciates him.

MORE AND MORE is DE PLUS EN PLUS…
Thus:

> Elle devient de plus en plus indiscrète
> et cramponne.
> She is getting more and more
> indiscreet and importunate.

MORE, meaning 'BESIDES,' 'MOREOVER,' is
DE PLUS (*pron.* de pluss).

WHAT IS MORE is rendered by QUI PLUS
EST…

MORE, meaning 'MORE NUMEROUS', is PLUS
NOMBREUX… *Thus:*

> Soyons sages. Ils sont plus nombreux
> que nous.
> Let us be careful. They are more than
> we are (there's more of them than
> of us).

SOME MORE is ENCORE DE…

To take 'SOME MORE' of a dish etc. (to take a
second helping) is REPRENDRE DE…

ONE MORE is ENCORE UN (UNE)...

ONE MORE meaning 'ONE OVER', 'ONE EXTRA', is UN DE PLUS.

'NO MORE!' (as an exclamation) is « ASSEZ ! »

ALL THE MORE is D'AUTANT PLUS.

THE MORE ... THE LESS ... is PLUS... MOINS... *Thus:*

> Plus vous gueulez, moins ils vous
> écoutent.
> The more you bawl, the less they
> listen to you

MORE OR LESS is PLUS OU MOINS. *Thus:*

> Elle est plus au moins toquée.
> She is more or less crazy.

NEITHER MORE NOR LESS is NI PLUS NI MOINS.

The final *s* of *plus* is sounded as *z* before a vowel or *h* mute; and as *ss* when *plus* stands either alone or at the end of a clause, or is used for the mathematical symbol 'plus.' In other cases it is not sounded at all.

« SUR »

Sur is a word of wonderful flexibility. You can scarcely write or speak good French without mastering its many shades of meaning. Here are a few.

It indicates *position*.—It may then mean 'on,' 'over,' 'in,' 'across,' 'to,' 'on the surface of,' 'against,' 'close to.' *Thus:*

> Elle s'abat sur le canapé.
> She flings herself on the sofa.

> Le nuage était sur nos têtes.
> The cloud was over our heads.

> Il inscrit son nom et adresse sur la fiche.
> He entered his name and address in
>   the registration-sheet.

> Les sapeurs ont jeté un pont sur la
>   Marne.
> The sappers have thrown a bridge
>   across the Marne.

> Je mets cela sur votre compte.
> I'm putting that down to your account.

> Aller sur mer, cela m'est affreux.
> Going to sea is terrible for me.

C'est le forgeron qui frappe sur
    l'enclume.
It's the blacksmith, hammering on
    (against) the anvil.

Stoppez sur le bord de la route.
Stop by (close to) the side of the road.

It indicates material or moral *ascendancy.*—
Thus:

Le roi règne sur plusieurs nationalités.
The King reigns over several nationalities.

Chez elle, la volonté l'emporte sur la
    raison.
In her case, strength of mind gets the
    better of reason.

It indicates *direction.*— *Thus:*

En tournant sur la droite, vous
    trouverez la maison.
If you turn to the right, you will find
    the house.

Sa chambre donna sur la terrasse.
Her room looked out on the terrace.

It indicates a *reversal of motion*.—

> Ils sont revenus sur leurs pas.
> They have retraced their steps.

It means *on the person*.—

> J'ai toujours un browning sur moi.
> I always carry a Browning (pistol).
>
> Elle avait toujours la lettre sur elle.
> She still had the letter on (or with)
>   her.

It indicates *tendency*, and *approximation*.—

> Ses yeux tirent sur le vert.
> Her eyes are greenish.
>
> Elle est sur le retour (d'âge).
> She is verging on the age of decline.
>
> Sur les onze heures.
> Towards 11 o'clock.
>
> Il va sur vingt ans.
> He is in his twentieth year.

It indicates *repetition*.—

>   Il a écrit et détruit lettre sur lettre.
>   He has written and destroyed letter
>   after letter.

>   Il faisait partir les plantons coup sur
>   coup.
>   He was sending off orderlies one after
>   the other.

It indicates *causation*, *sequence of ideas*, etc.—

>   Il ne faut pas juger cette affaire sur
>   les apparences.
>   You mustn't judge this affair on
>   appearances.

>   Elle cherche à s'excuser sur son
>   inexpérience.
>   She is trying to excuse herself on
>   account of her inexperience.

>   Il fait les habits sur commande.
>   He makes clothes to order.

It means *'out of'*.—

> Je retiendrai cela sur vos gages.
> I shall stop that out of your wages.

> Je la vois un jour sur trois, tout au plus.
> I see her one day out of three, at the
> very most.

> Sur les six œufs, il y en a deux qui
> sont pourris.
> Out of the six eggs, two are rotten.

> Trois fois sur quatre, il a raison.
> Three times out of four he is right.

It means *'about'*, *'concerning'*.—

> Elle l'a trompé sur ses intentions.
> She has misled him as to her intentions.

> Il ne voulait pas féliciter son ami sur
> son mariage.
> He did not want to congratulate his
> friend on his marriage.

> Ils se querellent sur des riens.
> They squabble over trifles.

And note the following.—

Prendre le pas sur...
To take precedence of ...

Avoir trois mètres sur cinq.
To measure 3 m by 5 m.

Prêter sur gages.
To lend against security or
    pledge.

Chanter (des paroles) sur l'air de...
To sing (words) to the tune of ...

Mettre quelqu'un sur un testament.
To mention (put) anyone in a will.

Sur le qui-vive.
On the look out.

Mettre une clef sur une porte.
To put a key in a lock of a door.

Pincer sur le fait.
To catch (anyone) in the act.

Sur ces entrefaites.
In the meantime.

Le prendre sur un ton haut.
To ride a high horse (be arrogant).

Quitter (quelqu'un) sur une poignée
    de mains.
To shake hands with someone and
    pass on.

Sur toutes choses.
Above all. Especially.

Sur ce, je vous fausse compagnie.
And now (without a word more) I
    must leave you.

La division marchait sur deux colonnes.
The division was moving in two columns.

Payer quelqu'un sur le pied de…
To pay anyone at the rate of …

Être sur pied.
To be ready, prepared.

Le blé sur pied.
Standing corn.

Sur le pied de guerre.
On a war-footing.

'HALF'

HALF, the noun, used in a precise sense, is rendered by LA MOITIÉ or LE DEMI. *Thus:*

> Trois est la moitié de six.
> Three is half (the half of) six.

> Deux demis font un entier.
> Two halves make a whole.

HALF, the noun, used loosely to mean 'quite a lot (of)' is rendered by LA MOITIÉ. *Thus:*

> La moitié du temps il est pompette !
> He is 'tight' (intoxicated) half the
>   time !

A HALF, meaning one half of a whole is UNE DEMIE. *Thus:*
> N'ayant pu en avoir un, j'en ai pris
>   une demie.
> As I couldn't get (a whole) one, I
>   took a half (one).

HALF, used loosely in the sense of 'partly,' 'incompletely,' is À DEMI or À MOITIÉ. *Thus:*

> Cette poire est à moitié pourrie.
> This pear is half rotten.

Il fait tout à demi.
He does everything by halves (skimps
   his work).

Elle était à demi morte.
She was half dead. (*Here*, 'Elle était
   demi-morte' would also be correct.)

HALF-WAY is À MOITIÉ CHEMIN or À MI-CHEMIN, the particle MI- being of course invariable.
HALF-PRICE is À MOITIÉ PRIX.

'HALF' applied to measures is always DEMI, never MOITIÉ.

DEMI as an adjective is invariable when it precedes the noun. When it follows the noun it agrees in gender, but remains in the singular. *Thus:*

Une demi-heure.
   But— À une heure et demie.
Une demi-bouteille.
   But— Trois bouteilles et demie.

A HALF-HOUR is UNE DEMIE. *Thus:*

J'ai entendu sonner la demie.
I heard the half-hour strike.

Cette pendule sonne les demies.
This clock strikes the half-hours.

C'est la demie de trois heures.
It is half past two (o'clock).

Demi- forming a compound noun or adjective is invariable. *Thus:*
>Une demi-lune ; des demi-lunes.
>Une demi-mesure ; des demi-mesures.
>Un demi-mal ; des demi-maux.
>>(A worry, a nuisance, but not so bad as it might have been.)
>Demi-fin (50% alloy) (*adj.*)

To go halves (with anyone) is Être de moitié avec quelqu'un. *Thus:*
>J'y suis de moitié avec vous.
>I'll go halves with you in that.

A verb following La moitié [or other similar quantitative noun such as *un quart* (a quarter), *un tiers* (one-third), *une douzaine* (a dozen), *une centaine* (about 100), etc.] is put in the singular if 'half' in a precise sense is intended. But if 'half' be used loosely to mean merely 'a lot (of)', or 'a high proportion (of)', then the verb is put in the plural. *Thus:*
>La moitié des otages est déjà morte.
>Half the hostages are already dead.

>La moitié de ses livres gisaient par terre.
>Half his books were lying on the ground.

COMPOUND ADJECTIVES

Adjectival compounds formed from two adjectives, or an adjective and a participle, are a common source of difficulty, especially as regards agreement and the use of the hyphen.

1. If the first adjective be used definitely as an adverb, it remains invariable, and the hyphen is always correct. *Thus:*

> Ces poulains sont court-jointés.
> These colts are (too) short in the
>   pastern.

> Les jeunes filles (et les dames mûres
>   également !) sont aujourd'hui
>   court-vêtues.
> Girls (and ladies of mature age
>   likewise!) are short-skirted today.

> Elles sont par surcroît court-bouclées.
> They are in addition 'bobbed.'

> Le garde-chasse a trouvé deux biches
>   nouveau-nées.
> The keeper has found two newly-born
>   roe deer (hinds).

The following are exceptions:

(a) Frais (meaning freshly) which always agrees with the preceding noun. *Thus:*

Je préfère les fraises fraîches cueillies.

I prefer strawberries freshly gathered.

(b) Grand in the expression Grand ouvert (wide open), which also agrees. *Thus:*

J'ai les yeux grands ouverts.

My eyes are wide open.

or

Elle a trouvé les deux fenêtres
grandes ouvertes.

She found both windows wide open.

In these two cases, and generally where the first of the adjectives is variable, it is better to omit the hyphen.

2. Certain compounds formed with Nouveau and a past participle (other than Nouveau-né above) are capable of application as both nouns and adjectives. *Such are:*

Nouveau venu ; Nouvel arrivé ;
Nouveau marié ; Nouveau converti ;
Nouveau riche.

In these cases both *nouveau* and the p.p. are variable, and the hyphen should be omitted.

3. Compounds indicative of mixed nationalities, or opposing nationalities, such as—

Anglo-saxon,
Franco-américain,
Russo-turc

may also be used as either nouns or adjectives. But here the second portion only is variable, and the hyphen must always be used.

4. Compound adjectives of colour are invariable, and are written without a hyphen.
Such are:

Bleu clair (light blue),
Châtain foncé (dark chestnut), etc.

Other adjectival expressions such as *gris de perle, vert et orange,* are likewise invariable, and hyphenless.

As a digression, whilst on the subject of colours, it is well to recall that where a French *noun* is used as an adjective of colour, it is invariable, the words *'couleur de'* being understood. *Such are:*

Azur,	Beige,	Carmin,	Cerise,
Lavande,	Marron,	Maïs (maize),	
Noisette,	Olive,	Paille,	
Ponceau (poppy),		Taupe (mole),	etc.

« TOUT »
AND ITS PECULIARITIES

Tout may be:

(1) An *adjective*, simple or indefinite, meaning 'all, each, every, whole, any.'

(2) An *indefinite pronoun*, meaning *'all, everything in general.'*

(3) A *noun*, meaning *'the (undivided) whole,'* or figuratively, *'the essential thing, the important thing.'*

(4) An *adverb*, meaning *'wholly, entirely, quite.'*

(5) Part of an *adverbial locution, e.g. 'tout à fait,'* meaning *'altogether.'*

Both in regard to its agreement and pronunciation it presents peculiar difficulties to the English mind.

(1) Tout as an Adjective

Used with article.—

Tout and Feu (the latter meaning 'late,' 'deceased') are the only adjectives which can precede the article.

Whereas, however, Feu is invariable when it precedes, Tout is variable. (Feu, of course, may follow a noun and article; note: *feu la reine* [or *'la feue reine'*] meaning 'the late queen.') *Thus:*

> Tous les hommes.
> All men (*or,* all the men).

> Toute la foule.
> The whole crowd.

> Toutes les femmes.
> All women (*or,* all the women).

> Toute une journée.
> A whole day long.

As to pronunciation, Tout (masc. sing.) is pronounced *tou* before a consonant, but *tout'* before a vowel or h mute. The masc. plural (Tous) is also pronounced *tou* when it commences a sentence or phrase, but *touss* at the end of a phrase, or when immediately preceding an adjective or a participle. *Thus:*

> À tout (*'tou'*) moment. —Incessantly.

Tout (*'tout'*) homme doit savoir que…
Every man should know that …

Tous (*'tou'*) les hommes ne sont pas
    sages.
All men (or, all the men) are not wise.

Sont-ils sages ? Ils ne le sont pas tous
    (*'touss'*).
Are they wise? Not all (of them) are.

Ils s'en vont tout (*'tou'*) fâchés.
They are going away quite (adverb)
    discontented.

Ils sont allés tous (*'touss'*)
    mécontents.
They went, all of them (adjective)
    discontented.

Used without article.—

As a simple adjective, presents no difficulty,
naturally agreeing with the following noun in
gender and number.

Toute femme doit être belle.
Every woman should be beautiful.

De toutes parts.
From all directions.

Used with 'GENS' (*meaning 'people'*).—
The general rule is that adjectives used with
GENS are put in the masculine, whether they
precede or follow that word (*Examples 1, 2*):

1. Je m'attends à trouver soupçonn*eux* ces
    gens-là.

    I expect to find these people
    suspicious.

2. Voilà des gens curi*eux*.

    There are some inquisitive folk.

but that an adjective *immediately* preceding,
together with any other adjectives that may
precede, is put in the feminine (*Examples 3, 4*):

3. Elle vient de visiter de *vieilles* gens.

    She has just been calling on some old
    people.

4. Voilà de bo*nnes* vie*illes* gens !

    There are some good old people!

though adjectives or past participles commencing
a sentence in which GENS is the subject follow
the general rule and remain in the masculine
(*Example 5*):

5. Rassur*és*, mais encore plain*tifs*, les
    vie*illes* gens, si ennuy*eux* jusque-là,
    rebroussèrent chemin.

    Reassured, but still grumbling, the old
    people, so annoying hitherto, turned
    back.

Also, where more than one adjective precedes
GENS, and the immediately-preceding adjective
has the same termination (usually -*e* mute) in
both masculine and feminine singular, the earlier
adjectives remain in the masculine (*Example 6*):

6.   Les vr*ais* honnêtes gens sont heureux.
     Real decent people are happy.

The above rather complicated set of rules and
exceptions should be studied bit by bit, referring
to the examples.

TOUT (or rather TOUS, since GENS is itself
plural) is, however, put in the masculine, whether
written before or after GENS (*Examples 7, 8*):

7.   *Tous* (*'tou'*) les gens vert*ueux* sont heur*eux*.
     All virtuous people are happy.

8.   Les gens prodigues sont *tous* (*'touss'*) malheur*eux*.
     Prodigal folk are all unhappy.

except that, if used with an adjective immediately
preceding GENS and therefore in the feminine
in accordance with the foregoing rules, it will
remain in the masculine if this adjective (in its
masculine singular) terminates in -*e* mute, and
will be put in the feminine in all other cases
(*Examples 9, 10*):

9.   Tous (*'tou'*) les *malhonnêtes* gens sont inqu*iets*.
     All dishonest people are uneasy.

10.   *Toutes* les *curieuses* gens sont act*ifs*.
        All inquisitive people are active.

   TOUT *as an indefinite adjective, meaning 'any',*
must always precede, and agree with, the noun.
Thus:
        Il vient à *toute* heure.
        He comes at any time.

   TOUT with 'AUTRE'.—
TOUT as an indefinite adjective with AUTRE
('TOUT AUTRE', meaning 'any other') must likewise
precede the noun. Thus used, TOUT varies if it
determines the noun that follows AUTRE. *Thus:*
        Je veux bien répondre à *toute* autre question.
        I am quite willing to answer any
            other question.

But if TOUT AUTRE be used adverbially,
meaning 'quite another,' this expression may
either precede or follow the noun, and in either
case TOUT remains invariable. *Thus:*
        Voici de *tout* autres affaires.
        Here (we have) quite other (totally
            different) business.

        C'est là une besogne tout autre.
        That is a job (of) quite another (kind).

Compare also the following:

1.   *Toute* autre femme l'aurait cru.
        Any other woman would have believed it.

2.   Mais cette fois j'ai affaire à une *tout*
            autre femme.
        But this time I have to deal with
            quite another (kind of) woman.

Tout with Place-names.—
Tout before a place-name (e.g. a town, used
with reference to all the inhabitants of the
place, or all its 'best society') remains invariable,
though the place-name be feminine. *Thus:*

1.   Le *tout*-Vienne a été content de
            savoir que…
        All Vienna (the Best People) has
            been glad to hear that …

2.   *Tout* Byzance y était.
        All Byzantium was at it.

On the other hand, if referring to the entire
area of the place, Tout would agree. Thus:
        Toute Rome est aujourd'hui couverte
            de neige.
        The whole of Rome is covered with
            snow to-day.

'Tout,' 'Chaque,' 'Tous Les…' meaning 'every.'—

There is a subtle distinction between Tout and Chaque. Tout is employed in a comprehensive sense, the whole being viewed without consideration of its component parts. Chaque is used in the sense of passing in review each individual component constituting the whole. *Thus:*

1.   *Tout ('tout'')* homme est mortel.
      Every man (all mankind) is mortal.

2.   *Chaque* soldat touchera cette
        gratification.
      Every (each individual) soldier will
        receive this allowance.

'Tous (toutes) les…' may also involve a subtlety. *Thus:*
      Tous les mois de l'année n'ont pas un
        nombre identique de jours.
      Every month of the year has not an
        equal number of days.

On the other hand:
      Il vient tous les mois.
      He comes every month
        (implying only one visit per month).

(2) TOUT AS AN INDEFINITE PRONOUN

As an indefinite pronoun, meaning 'all,' 'everything (in general),' TOUT is of course invariable, and follows directly after a verb in a simple tense, but is placed between the auxiliary and the past participle in the compound tenses.

With the infinitive of a verb, it may precede or follow, the former being as a rule preferable. *Thus:*

> Je disais tout.
> I was telling everything.

> J'ai tout dit.
> I have told everything.

> Il faut tout dire.
> Everything must be told.

(NOTE— 'RIEN', meaning 'nothing,' follows the same rules.)

(3) TOUT AS A NOUN

TOUT as a noun may mean 'the entity,' 'the whole.' In this sense it has a plural (TOUTS).

Examples:

1. Le tout est plus grand que la partie.
    The whole is greater than a part.

2. Il y avait plusieurs touts distincts.
   There were several distinct entities.

Or, it may mean 'the essential,' 'the most important,' thing. *Thus:*

3. Le tout est de vous reposer.
   The most important thing is for you
   to rest.

(4) Tout as an Adverb

Tout as an adverb, meaning 'wholly,' 'entirely,' 'quite,' 'all,' is remarkable in that it is *variable* before a feminine adjective or participle commencing with a consonant or *h* aspirate (*Examples 1, 2, 3, 4*):

1. Je vous le dis *tout* net (*pron.* net').
   I tell you quite plainly.

2. Ils sont partis *tout* contents.
   They left quite happy.

3. Elle a été *tout* (*pron.* tout') heureuse
       (*h* mute).
   She was quite happy.

4. Elle a été *toute h*onteuse (*h* aspirate).
   She was quite ashamed.

5.   Elle se plaint de ce que son fiancé
          porte les cravates *toutes* faites.
     She complains of her fiancé wearing
          ready-made ties.

6.   J'ai horreur des vêtements *tout* faits.
     I loathe ready-made clothes.

The like rule holds if, instead of an adjective or participle, we have a phrase equivalent thereto (*Examples 7, 8*):

7.   J'ai vu Suzanne *tout* en larmes.
     I saw Suzanne quite tearful.

8.   J'ai là une boîte *toute* d'acier.
     I have there a box all (made of) steel.

But if used adverbially immediately before a noun, TOUT never varies, and incidentally must be repeated before each of successive nouns. *Thus:*

     Cette étoffe est *tout* laine.
     This stuff is all (pure) wool.

     Ces murs sont *tout* yeux et *tout*
          oreilles.
     These walls are all eyes and ears.

It is necessary to discriminate carefully between the adjectival and the adverbial sense, when using TOUT with an adjective or participle. *Thus:*

1. (*Adject.*) —Ces pensées sont *toutes* aussi fraîches qu'hier.

   These pansies are *all* (of them) as fresh as (they were) yesterday.

2. (*Adverb*) —Ces pâquerettes sont *tout* aussi fraîches qu'hier.

   These daisies are *quite* as fresh as (they were) yesterday.

3. (*Adject.*) —L'église était *toute* en feu.

   The church was all (all of it) on fire.

   (This conveys the idea that the whole edifice was involved.)

4. (*Adverb*) —La maison était *tout* en feu.

   The house was quite on fire (well alight).

   (This expresses the idea that the flames had got a strong hold, but that the entire building was not yet in flames.)

Tout—que

Tout as an adverb, followed by an adjective and Que, meaning 'however —,' is similar to *quelque — que*, and *si — que*, which have a like meaning.

When so used, Tout is variable before a feminine adjective or participle commencing with a consonant or *h* aspirate. But the verb following must be in the INDICATIVE, whereas both *quelque — que* and *si — que* require the SUBJUNCTIVE. The reason is that Tout — que is more strongly affirmative, indicates experience, and excludes the ideas of doubt or uncertainty. *Thus:*

1. *Tout* redoutables *que sont* ces vices...
    However formidable these vices *are* ...

2. *Toutes* puissantes *que sont* ces reines barbares...
    However powerful these barbaric queens *are* ...

But—3. *Si* habile *qu'*il *soit* il ne réussira pas.
    However skilled *he (may) be* he will not succeed.

And—4. *Quelque* riches *qu'*ils *soient* ...
    However rich they *may be* ...

Tout Compounded with Adjectives

Tout- compounded with an adjective, meaning 'all- —,' *e.g. 'tout-puissant'* ('all-powerful,' 'almighty'), is peculiar in its masculine plural, which is written *'tout-puissants'*. The feminine singular is *'toute-puissante'*, and the feminine plural *'toutes-puissantes'*.

Tout Compounded with Nouns

The principal compounds in use are *toute-bonne,* a variety of the plant sage, and also a variety of pear; and *toute-épice,* allspice. Plural *toutes- —s,* in both cases.

'Tout-ensemble', so frequently met with in English, is not really used in French.

(5) Tout in Locutions

Some of the more common locutions are as follows:

Du tout, equivalent to *'nullement'*, meaning: 'not at all,' often used in polite reassurances.

Pas (point) du tout : Not at all.

Tout à fait :	Altogether.
Tout de bon :	In real earnest.
Tout à coup :	All of a sudden.
Tout d'un coup :	All at once; all at a blow.
Tout de go :	Straight out; bluntly; unceremoniously.
Tout à l'heure :	In a moment; presently.
Tout au moins :	At the very least.
Tout au plus :	At the very most.
En tout :	On the whole.
En tout cas :	In any case; whatever happens.
Par-dessus tout :	Above all.
Une fois pour *toutes* :	Once (and) for all.
Toutes les fois que... :	As often as... ; every time...
À toutes jambes :	At full speed.
Tout à vous (toi) :	At your service; devotedly yours.
C'est tout un :	That's all the same, all one.
C'est tout comme :	That's much the same thing.
« Tout-beau ! » :	'Steady!' (to restrain dogs, hounds, etc.)

sense of *within* or *inside* is not stressed. But as
certain names of towns and villages themselves
include the article, Au or À la must of course
be written in such cases:

> Ils allaient à Rouen.
> They were going to Rouen.

> Elle restait à Paris.
> She remained in Paris.

> J'irai *au* Caire cet hiver.
> I shall go to Cairo this winter.

Dans (with Place-names)

Dans is used with the names of the following
territories, irrespective of gender, all of which
require the article, *viz.:*

1. States of the U.S.A. and Mexico.— These
may be of either gender.

> Des inondations sérieuses se sont pro-
> duites *dans l'*Illinois (*pron.* Ill-in-oâ).
> Serious floods have occurred in Illinois.

2. British and Irish Counties.— These are all
masculine.

> On signale un tremblement de terre
> *dans le* Yorkshire.
> An earthquake is reported in Yorkshire.

En (with Place-names)

1. Before names of countries or provinces, wherever situated, of feminine gender [these as a rule are used without an article, but *for exceptions see page 138 following*]:

> J'ai fait sa connaissance *en* Afrique.
> (*Or, more properly:* J'ai fait connaissance avec lui.)
> I made his acquaintance in Africa.

2. Before names of countries or provinces, within Europe, of masculine gender and not used with the article:

> Il a demeuré *en* Danemark depuis quelques années.
> He has lived in Denmark for some years.

> Sa tante est en Anjou.
> His aunt is in Anjou.

À (with Place-names)

Before names of countries or provinces, outside Europe, of masculine gender and used with the article:

> Il a trouvé un emploi quelconque *au* Brésil.
> He has found some sort of a job in Brazil.

> Un froid anormal sévit *au* Canada.
> Abnormal cold afflicts Canada.

L'automne (*pron.* ô-tone) est charmant
    aux États-Unis.
Autumn is charming in the United States.

Dᴀɴꜱ *or* Eɴ (ᴡɪᴛʜ Pʟᴀᴄᴇ-ɴᴀᴍᴇꜱ)
Dᴀɴꜱ—with names of countries or provinces
within Europe, of masculine gender and used
with the article:
    J'ai fait une tournée *dans le* Hanovre.
    I have made a trip in Hanover.
If, in common parlance, the article be omitted,
then Eɴ must be used, *e.g.—en Portugal.* The
article is usually insisted upon in the case of
Hanovre, more license being used with other parts.

Dᴀɴꜱ *or* À (ᴡɪᴛʜ Pʟᴀᴄᴇ-ɴᴀᴍᴇꜱ)
À—before the names of certain islands, usually
written without either the article or the word
Îʟᴇ. If, however, the word Îʟᴇ be used, then
Dᴀɴꜱ ʟ'Îʟᴇ — must of course be employed.

    Il possede une belle propriété *à* Cuba.
    He owns a fine property in Cuba.

    Son fils a des intérêts importants *dans
        l'île* de la Réunion.
    His son has important interests in the
        island of Réunion.

Dans *or* À, according to the meaning.—
The following countries, territories, etc., some of
which are of feminine gender, are always to be
written with the article. In their case Dans (*in,
into, to*) or À (*in, to, at*) must be used according
to the sense.

Les Açores.	La Jamaïque.
Les Antilles.	Le Japon.*
L'Ascension.	Le Maroc.
La Barbade.	La Martinique.
Le Bengale.	Le Mexique.
Le Brésil.	Le Nicaragua.
Le Canada.	(Territories
Le Chili.	compounded with
Les États-Unis.*	Nouveau- or
La Grande-	Nouvelle-).*
Bretagne,	Le Paraguay.
Le Groenland	Les Pays-Bas.
(*pron.* Grin-lan).	Le Pérou.
La Guadeloupe.	Les Philippines.
Le Guatemala.	La Plata.
La Guyane.	La Réunion.
Les Hébrides.	Le Tibet (le Thibet).
L'Inde.	La Trinité.
Les Indes.*	

N.B.—The *capital* of Mexico is not 'Mexique',
but Mexico, in French.
* In these cases À or Aux is usually preferable.

DANS & EN, WITH FRENCH DEPARTMENTS.—

These may be of either gender.

Certain French Departments are *compound* names, singular or plural, masculine or feminine. In these cases, DANS LE may be used when the first of the compound names is masculine; DANS LA when it is feminine; DANS LES when it is plural. Alternatively, one may write, DANS LE DÉPARTEMENT DE — ; or one may omit the article, and write EN —. *Thus:*

> Elle à acheté un château *dans le* Calvados (*pron.* Cal-va-doss).
> —She has bought a country house in Calvados.

> Il a liquidé ses propriétés *dans les* Bouches-du-Rhône et acquis un terrain *en* Seine-et-Oise.
> —He has disposed of his properties in the Bouches-du-Rhône and acquired some land in Seine-et-Oise.

Of the French départements, VAUCLUSE is unique in *not* being written with the article. In this case, EN must be used instead of DANS.

[Note.—The ancient provinces of France do not follow the rules applicable to the modern départements noted above. *Therefore:*

    Cet été, j'irai *en* Touraine.
    This summer, I shall go to Touraine.]

DANS AND EN EXPRESSING TIME

DANS implies 'after,' 'after the expiration of…'
EN implies 'during.' *Thus:*

    Il le fera *dans* une semaine.
    He will do it in a week's time. (He will
        begin to do it a week from now.)

    Il le fera *en* une semaine.
    He will do it in a week. (It will take him
        a week to do it, whenever he begins.)

DANS MEANING 'OUT OF'

Paradoxically, DANS corresponds to the English
'out of' in such expressions as:

    Manger *dans* une assiette.
    To eat out of (off) a plate.

    Boire *dans* une bouteille.
    To drink out of a bottle.

« OUI, NON, SI, NE…PAS, POINT »

Sı replaces Ouı in reply to a negative-interrogative, or to contradict a negative statement. *Examples:*

> Vous ne me remettez pas ?
> You don't remember me?
> — Mais *si* ; c'est Adèle !
> — Yes I do! It's Adèle!

> Alors, vous ne l'avez pas revu ?
> So, you did not see him again?
> — *Si.* Je l'ai revu à Londres.
> — Yes, I did! I saw him in London.

And note the following:

> Vous dites que *non* ; moi, je dis que *si.*
> You say no (it isn't); I say yes (it is).

> Vous dites que *oui* ; moi, je dis que *non.*
> You say yes (it is); I say no (it isn't).

> Elle n'est pas déjà partie ?
> She hasn't gone already?
> — Je crois que *si. Si fait.*
> — I think she has. Yes, indeed she has.

Non cannot negative a verb.

NENNI (*pron.* na-ni) may be used familiarly in place of NON, and both it and OUI may be reinforced by -DA (-DÀ). *Thus:*

Nenni-da !
Not at all! By no means!

Oui-da !
Oh yes! Rather! Oh dear, yes!

NON, at the end of a sentence, may replace 'N'EST-CE PAS ?':

Ça ne te fait rien, non ?
That doesn't matter to you, does it?

PAS and POINT are usually adjuncts of NE, which they supplement and reinforce.

POINT is more emphatic than PAS.
NE…POINT rather corresponds to the English 'not a jot'; 'not a bit.' *Examples:*

Il ne parle pas.
He isn't speaking.

Il ne parle point.
He doesn't speak (never speaks).

POINT cannot be used before BEAUCOUP, and is only rarely used before TROP.

PAS should be used before NUMBERS, also before comparatives such as SI, PLUS, MOINS, AUTANT.

In interrogative-negatives, PAS and POINT convey subtle distinctions of meaning, thus PAS may convey the idea of surprise or reproach; POINT the idea of doubt. *Examples:*

> Ne l'avez-vous *pas* vu ?
> Didn't you see him? (Do you mean to tell me you didn't see him?)

> N'est-ce *point* vous qui le regardiez ?
> Wasn't it you who were looking at him?

POINT may replace NON in the following cases:

1. In ellipsis, i.e. where a word or words are 'understood.' *Thus:*
> Je la croyais maligne, mais *point*.
> I thought she was clever, but she isn't.

2. As an emphatic negative to a direct enquiry. *Thus:*
> Voulez-vous le recevoir ?
> Will you see him?
>> —Point !
>> —Certainly not!

There are certain cases in which PAS or POINT *may* be (and usually are) omitted, and other cases in which they *must* be omitted, leaving NE standing alone before the verb. Often the omission is accounted for by the presence of some other word or phrase of equivalent import.

Omission of PAS or POINT is usual—

1. After the verbs SAVOIR, POUVOIR, OSER, CESSER, IMPORTER.
Examples:

> Je ne puis le supporter.
> I cannot stand it.

> Il ne sait se taire.
> He does not know how to keep his
>   mouth shut.

> Il n'osa aborder la dame.
> He dared not accost the lady.

> Elle ne cesse de larmoyer.
> She never stops blubbing.

> Ça n'importe.
> That doesn't matter.

But—in the case of Savoir, if complete ignorance is intended to be conveyed, then Pas or Point is retained. *Thus:*

> Mon gendre (*pron.* jan-dre) ne sait
> *point* le latin.
> My son-in-law knows no Latin.

> Il ne sait *pas* ce qu'il fait.
> He doesn't know what he is doing.

But—

> Il *ne* sait ce qu'il fait.
> He does not realize what he is doing. (He is acting at random, without purpose.)

2. After such expressions as Si ce n'est ; Si ce n'était ; N'était ; N'eût été, meaning 'were it not for', 'had it not been for', 'but for.'

3. After Pour que, meaning 'lest.' *Example:*

> File, pour que je ne t'envoie une gifle !
> Off with you, or I might land you a
> smack in the face !

4. After Il y a meaning 'it is'; or Depuis que, meaning 'since,' when the verb following is in the perfect or pluperfect indicative. *Thus:*

> Il y a une semaine que je ne lui ai parlé.
> It is a week since I (last) spoke to him.

But if the verb following be in the present or imperfect, then PAS or POINT must be retained. *Thus:*

> J'ai été triste depuis que nous *ne* nous
> voyons *pas*.
> I've been sad since we (no longer) see
> one another.

5. After IL N'Y A POINT meaning 'there is no...'; and with AUCUN, PERSONNE, or similar negatives. *Thus:*

> Il n'y a point d'homme qui ne soit de
> temps en temps de mauvaise humeur.
> There is no man who is not cross now
> and then.

> Je ne vois personne qui ne pense ainsi.
> Everyone I see thinks so.

6. After VOICI or VOILÀ with an expression of time. *Thus:*

> Voilà six mois que je n'en ai de nouvelles.
> It is six months now since I had news
> of them.

7. In the expression N'AVOIR D'AUTRE...QUE... *Thus:*

> Je n'ai d'autre intention que de rester.
> I have no intention of leaving (no
> intention except to stay).

But—if AUTRE is omitted and is to be understood, then PAS or POINT *must* also be omitted. *Thus:*

> Il n'a de dispositions que pour le
> théâtre.
> The only inclinations he has are for
> the theatre.

8. With expressions of time preceded by DE. *Thus:*

> Elle a juré de ne lui pardonner de la vie.
> She has sworn never to forgive him as
> long as she lives.

9. After PRENDRE GARDE QUE, 'take care lest.' *Thus:*

> Prends garde qu'on ne t'attrape.
> Take care you aren't caught.

BUT, if PRENDRE GARDE is used in the sense of 'observe, take note,' then the following verb must be in the indicative and not the subjunctive, and PAS or POINT must be retained. *Thus:*

> Prenez garde que ce témoin ne *dit* pas
> la vérité.
> Take note that this witness is not
> speaking the truth.

But—

Prenez garde qu'il ne *dise* la vérité !
Take care he doesn't (lest he) speak the
truth !

10. Note the following subtleties:

Y a-t-il donc rien dont il *ne* se plaint ?
Is there anything he doesn't complain of ?
(Here a negative answer is obviously
expected.)

Y a-t-il personne (ou quelqu'un) ici
qui *n'ait pas* encore reçu sa carte
d'identité ?
Is there anyone here who has not yet
received his Identity Card ?
(Here the questioner is genuinely
uncertain, and there is no negative
suggestion implied.)

Omission of 'Pas' or 'Point' is Obligatory—

1. Where the sentence includes any following, *viz.:*

Personne; nul:	Nobody; no one.
Aucun :	None; no one.
Aucunement :	Not at all.
Rien :	Nothing.
Jamais :	Never.
Plus :	More.
Guère :	Not much; scarcely.
Goutte :	A drop.
Qui (Quoi) que ce soit :	Anyone (anything) at all.

Examples:

Personne ne s'en occupe.
No one troubles about it.

Nul n'est prophète en son pays.
Nobody is a prophet in his own country.

Aucun n'est content de son sort.
No one is content with his lot.

Je ne m'y fie aucunement.
I don't rely upon it at all.

Vous ne faites rien pour savoir.
You are not doing anything to find out.

Il ne vient jamais le dimanche.
He never comes on Sundays.

Je n'ai plus d'argent.
I have no more money.

[But— *observe the following subtleties:*

Je n'ai plus de billets de mille francs.
I have no more 1000-franc notes.

Je n'ai *pas* plus de mille francs.
I have not got more than 1000 francs.]

Dernièrement, je ne la vois guère.
Latterly, I scarcely (ever) see her.

Il ne boit goutte.
He doesn't drink a drop.

Je ne quête quoi que ce soit.
I'm not looking for anything at all.
    (Note— Quêter implies rather
    begging or cadging, *e.g.* for alms,
    votes, etc. It is also used in the
    sense of seeking *game*.)

2. After Savoir in the conditional, used instead
   of Pouvoir. *Thus:*
   > Je ne saurais vous dire.
   > I couldn't (can't) tell you.

3. When two negatives are connected by Ni.
   Thus:
   > Sa mère ne lit ni n'ecrit.
   > Her (his) mother neither reads nor
   > writes.

4. In the case of the phrase Ne… que, meaning
   'only'. *Thus:*
   > Il ne leur manque que la bonne volonté.
   > All they lack is good will.

5. In the rather rare and literary case of a
   sentence commencing with Que—, used
   for Pourquoi—, and expressing regret,
   reproach, etc.:
   > Que n'êtes-vous donc parti ?
   > Why have you not gone ?

BELGIAN FRENCH

BEWARE OF 'BELGIAN FRENCH!' It is no disparagement of our gay, gallant and honourable allies to point out that, in the nature of things, the French language has become greatly modified, and even distorted, in their charming country.

Pure French is spoken and written in cultured circles, but the popular idiom is a very different matter. One may be able to understand it, yet be wholly unable to speak it. And the worst of it is that the Belgian uses French words in a totally different sense from the French sense. He will, for example, use *savoir* to express the French *pouvoir*, and *connaître* as equivalent to *savoir*. He will, without a blush, make *si* govern the conditional mood, substitute *être* for *avoir* and say *septante* for *soixante-dix*, *nonante* for *quatre-vingt-dix*, *etc.*

Hence, mistakes and misunderstandings are apt to arise, which may be trivial, serious, or merely ludicrous. Once upon a time, a perfectly respectable French father of a family was at a loss to explain the coolness with which he was received amongst his friends in Brussels. He had announced at luncheon, with paternal satisfaction:

J'ai *marié* ma fille le mois dernier.

I married my daughter last month.

Alas! to a Belgian *'marier'* and *'épouser'* are *kif-kif* (the same thing), and poor Papa had innocently accused himself of incest!

Remember, therefore:
MARIER, *v.a.* To marry, match, give in marriage. (Also, to blend, join, unite—colours, sounds, ropes, etc.)

SE MARIER, *v.pr.** To get (be) married [**v pr.: verbe pronominal (reflexive)*].

ÉPOUSER, *v.a.* To wed. (Also, figuratively, to espouse or conform closely to.)

NOTE [2010]— The addressing of envelopes is currently different for Belgium and France. Generally in France (see also page 263 following) the house or building number appears *before* the street name *without* a comma (in Luxembourg the same order applies *with* a comma); while in Belgium (as also in Switzerland) the number appears *after* the street name, without a comma, *e.g.*—

Mlle Jeanne Ribot	Mlle Jeanne Ribot
Rue Archimède 73	288 boulevard Saint-Germain
1000 Bruxelles	75007 PARIS
BELGIQUE	FRANCE

PART VI

MORE TABLE TALK
Autres propos de table

236 idiomatic sentences
236 phrases idiomatiques

More 'table talk.' —You can open it anywhere, and learn something.

AUTRES PROPOS DE TABLE

1. Monsieur le comte est complètement *brouillé avec* la petite N—.
2. Il se rendait *compte* des dangers qu'offrait cette liaison.
3. Il entendait *se défiler en douce.*

4. Devant cette explosion, il se décida *à filer doux.*
5. J'ai rencontré les A— et les B— *de compagnie.*
6. Alors, *vous voilà arrivé !* Et *comment c'est Paris ?*
7. Je passe justement par là. Puis-je vous *pousser un bout ?*
8. Il paraît *que* c'est être déjà vieux aujourd'hui *que* de *toucher à la quarantaine.*
9. Il m'*en arrive une bien bonne !* Je vais te *la* raconter *de toi à moi.*
10. *L'on* s'empara de lui et *l'on* le conduisit *au poste.*
11. Auriez-vous la bonté de mettre ces lettres *à la poste* en passant ?
12. Il partit en *faisant claquer* la porte.

13. Elle a tout de même *de quoi* me plaire.

14. *Enfoncez*-vous bien cela dans la tête !

1. The Count has completely fallen out with the little N— woman.
2. He realized the dangers this entanglement involved.
3. He meant to slip away quietly.

4. In face of this explosion, he decided to lie low.
5. I met the A—s and the B—s going about together.
6. So here you are! And how's Paris?

7. I'm just going that way. Can I give you a lift?
8. It seems that to be verging on the forties is to be already old, nowadays.
9. A nice thing's happened to me! I'll tell you about it, strictly between ourselves.
10. They seized on him and led him off to the police station.
11. Would you be so kind as to post these letters on your way?
12. He went off, banging the door.

13. All the same she has something about her that I like.
14. Get that well into your head!

15. C'est M. Brown, un des *rares* anglais qui *aient* réussi aux États-Unis.

16. Dans cette affaire, je ne suis pas *à la page*.

17. Avant de décider *quoi que ce soit*, vous me mettrez au courant.

18. Monique *est à traire* les vaches.

19. *Si qu'*on *irait* se coucher ?

20. —La propriété de Monsieur de R— n'est pas loin ?
    —C'est la *grille tout de suite* sur la route.*
    (* Very ungrammatical, of course!)

21. Le délit qu'elle a commis n'est pas *de ceux qui* font *montrer du doigt* celles qui s'en sont rend*ues* coupables.

22. Elle *sortait* un petit coffre de *son* nécessaire.

23. —Elle est slave ?
    —Je ne sais pas. Il y a *quelque chose de* slave *dans son cas*, cela se voit.

24. Je n'ai pas encore l'âge de me coucher comme les poules, *que je sache !*

25. Le vrai *snob* n'est pas celui qui, ayant tracé sur le sol un cercle, déclare « vivre hors d'ici n'est pas vivre »… c'est celui qui *s'efforce de* pénétrer *dans* le cercle.

15. That's Mr Brown, one of the few Englishmen who have made good in the United States.
16. I'm not in the know about this business.

17. Before deciding anything at all, you'll let me know.
18. Monica is busy milking the cows.

19. Supposing we went to bed? (A colloquialism, ungrammatical.)
20. —Monsieur de R—'s place isn't far, is it?

    —It's the gate just down the road.

21. The offence she has committed is not one of those that causes *women* guilty of them to be pointed at.
22. She took a little box out of her hand-bag.

23. —Is she a Slav?
    —I don't know. There's something Slav about her, that can be seen.
24. I'm still not of an age, so far as I know, to go to roost with (at the same time as) the hens!
25. The real snob is not the one who, having drawn a circle on the ground, gives out that 'living outside this is not living at all' … it is the one who endeavours to wriggle into the circle. (NOTE— *Pénétrer*, as a neuter verb, conveys the idea of *struggling*.)

26. —Tu t'amuses, les week-ends, dans ta chaumière ?

    —Oui-dà, chérie, mais à vrai dire je trouve le *cheptel* assez *bruyant* ! Il y a les coqs qui *chantent* ; les poules qui *gloussent* ; les bœufs et les vaches qui *beuglent* et qui *mugissent* ; les moutons et les brebis qui *bêlent* ; une jument qui *hennit* (*pron.* hè-ni) ; des ânes et des ânesses qui *braient* ; et les chiens qui *aboient*. Tout ça ne finit pas !

    —N'as-tu pas de chat qui *miaule* ?

27. Sa *marotte* finira bien par lui passer.

28. Ne savez-vous donc pas reconnaître votre droite de votre gauche ?

29. —Elle est *à couteaux tirés* avec ce bon Gaspard.

    —Oui, mais elle a l'air bien *emballé sur* le jeune Max !

30. Je suis *désolé de* vous avoir *fait attendre*. Y a-t-il longtemps que vous êtes là ?

31. Ne *vous en faites* donc pas pour ça !

32. Il commence à *mettre des bâtons dans les roues*.

33. —Il faut que je *me sauve*. On m'attend.

    —Au revoir. Tâche d'*être rentré à* une heure.

34. Je ne *tire* rien d'elle que des réponses indécises.

26. —Do you enjoy yourself, at week-ends, in your cottage?

    —Rather! darling, but truth to tell I find the livestock pretty noisy! There are cocks that crow; hens that cluck; bullocks and cows that low and bellow; sheep and ewes that bleat; a mare that neighs; donkeys and lady-donkeys that bray; and dogs that bark. There's no end to it!

    —Haven't you a cat that mee-ows?

27. That monomania of his will leave him in the end.

28. Don't you know your right from your left?

29. —She is at daggers drawn with our friend Gaspard.

    —Yes, but she seems very gone on young Max!

30. I'm fearfully sorry for having kept you waiting. Have you been *here* long?

31. Don't you worry about that!

32. He is beginning to raise objections.

33. —I must fly. They're waiting for me.

    —Au revoir. (See you.) Try to be back by one o'clock.

34. I can't get anything out of her, except indecisive answers.

35. Je *change* tout de même avec lui !

36. Ce petit *bibi fait valoir* ma nouvelle redingote.

37. C'était la patronne de l'auberge qui sortit de *sa* chambre, son bougeoir à *la* main, et des *papillotes* tout autour de la tête.

38. Vous n'*avez qu'à* téléphoner ! Le téléphone n'est pas fait pour les chiens, je suppose !

39. Il fait un temps de chien, *c'est tout juste si* je ne *claque* pas *des dents.*

40. Allons donc *bouffer au Claridge !*

41. Pourquoi *courir* si vite ?

42. Les chevaux *font* de gros prix aujourd'hui.

43. Il *mettait un point d'honneur à* ne répandre que des histoires fidèles.

44. Elle portait un petit paquet *enveloppé de papier de soie.*

45. Au bourg (*pron.* bour) je me suis *jeté dans* la femme du notaire.

46. Ce serait un joli *gâchis, que* de leur dévoiler ce secret.

47. Elle est très *fréquentable.*

48. Elle *mène* très bien *sa barque.*

35. All the same I wouldn't mind changing places with him!

36. This little hat shows off my new coat.

37. It was the proprietress of the inn that came out of her bedroom, candlestick in hand, and curl-papers all round her head. (NOTE— *Chambre* means, in particular, a *bedroom*.)

38. You've only to telephone! The telephone wasn't made for nothing (was made to be used), I suppose!

39. It's rotten weather, my teeth are jolly near chattering.

40. Let's go and feed at Claridge's.

41. Why run so fast?

42. Horses are fetching big prices just now.

43. He made it a point of honour to spread only true yarns.

44. She was carrying a little parcel wrapped in tissue-paper.

45. In the (market-) town I ran right into the notary's wife.

46. A nice mess it would make of things, to reveal that secret to them.

47. She is quite a good sort to be with.

48. She manages her affairs very cleverly.

49. Vite ! *Amène-toi !* On va *rater* le plus beau !
50. *Pour quand*, ce *dîner prié ?*

51. C'est un boxeur, et ce qu'on fait de mieux dans le genre. Il est champion des *poids mi-lourds.*
52. Le *coup d'envoi* est pour 3 h.

53. L'équipe française a *marqué* 10 points à 6.

54. Ce n'est pas *la mer à boire, que* de faire ça.

55. Tu *pêches un compliment !*

56. *Voici venir* l'hiver. Il sera, dit-on, rig*ou*reux.

57. Qu'y a-t-il encore *de cassé ?*

58. Nous sommes rentrés à Paris *par le train.*

59. Il est revenu en Europe *sur* le *Berengaria.*

60. Nous irons *avec* l'auto.

61. À Cannes il y a une grande *affluence* d'*hivernants.*
62. Ça fait mauvais effet. Ça risque d'*attrouper* les personnes.
63. Marie *se prit à* pleurer.

49. Quick! Buck up! We shall miss the best of it!

50. When is it, this dinner-party?
    (NOTE—*Un dîner prié* is a regular dinner-party, for which formal invitations are sent out.)

51. He is a boxer, and one of the best of his kind. He is middle-weight champion.

52. The kick-off is at three o'clock.

53. The French team has scored 10 points against 6.

54. It isn't such a terrible thing after all, to do that.

55. You're fishing! (for a compliment).

56. Here is winter coming. It will be, they say, a hard one.

57. What's gone wrong now?

58. We returned to Paris by train.

59. He returned to Europe *in* the *Berengaria*.

60. We'll go in the car.

61. At Cannes there is a great crowd of winter visitors.

62. That makes a bad impression. It runs the risk of collecting a whole crowd of people.

63. Marie started to cry.

64. Ce décor est *d'*un peintre *et qui* sait son métier.

65. Elle s'était souve*nue* à temps du dîner *où* elle était *conviée* chez les *Michaud*.

66. Je t'enverrai tes *affaires, en colis restant*.

67. Il est *attaché d'*ambassade, *détaché au* ministère des affaires étrangères.

68. Aujourd'hui je me trouve dans une *contre-passe* fâcheuse.

69. Entre *copains,* l'aimable familiarité est *de mise*.

70. —*Un* verre de madère ?
    —*Ce n'est pas de refus.*

71. Je ne me souviens plus *de* son nom.

72. Elle mordillait nerveusement *son fume-cigarette*.

73. Vous verrez la dédicace sur la *page de garde*.

74. Bas les pattes ! Je te défends ! Je *le* dirai à Françoise !

75. On dirait que tu *roulais sur l'or*. Où *prendras*-tu l'argent ?

76. J'ai imaginé cette histoire *de bout en bout*.

77. Je n'ai pas déjà *de* si bons yeux.

64. This scenery is (done) by an artist (painter), one who knows his job.
65. She remembered in time the dinner-party at the Michaud's, to which she had been invited.
66. I'll send you on your kit, as a parcel to be called for.
67. He is an Embassy attaché, (temporarily) attached to the Ministry of Foreign Affairs.
68. Today I'm in an annoying predicament.

69. Between pals, an amiable familiarity is quite allowable. (NOTE— *Copain*, *fem.: copine.*)
70. —Have a glass of Madeira?
    —I can't say no.
71. I've utterly forgotten his (her) name.

72. She was nervously nibbling her cigarette-holder.
73. You'll see the dedication on the fly-leaf.

74. Paws off! I forbid you! I'll tell Françoise!

75. One would think you were rolling in wealth. Where are you going to get the money from?
76. I made up that yarn from beginning to end.
77. My eyesight is none too good as it is.

78. Je suis toujours levée *à* sept heures.

79. Et *quand cela serait*, il aurait du résister.

80. Nous avons *tout le temps*.

81. —Je m'appelle Alice Girard, et je suis née rue de R—, à Paris.
    —Alors, *nous sommes pays*. Moi aussi je suis né rue de R—.

82. Votre *voisin de gauche* est Dupin, le sénateur.

83. Elle m'a *pris en grippe*.

84. Après le déjeuner, je mets un vieux chapeau, je *passe un* imperméable, et je file à la gare.

85. C'est pas vrai ! Tu me *montes un bateau !*

86. —Sais-tu où elle allait ?
    —Non. Comment *veux-tu* que *je sache ?*

87. Je préfère *être en pays de connaissance*.

88. Il est neuf heures *à* ma montre.

89. Il ne faut jamais *conclure du particulier au général*.

90. On apprend *à tout âge*.

91. *Par où* y va-t-on ?

78. I'm always up by seven o'clock.

79. And even if it were so, he should have resisted.

80. We have heaps of time.

81. —I'm called Alice Girard, and I was born in the rue de R—, in Paris.
    —Then we are from the same parts. I also was born in the rue de R—.

82. Your left-hand neighbour is Dupin, the senator.

83. She has taken a dislike to me.

84. After lunch, I put on an old hat, slipped on a mackintosh, and flew off to the station.

85. It's not true! You're pulling my leg!

86. —Do you know where she was going to?
    —No. How do you suppose I should know?

87. I prefer to be amongst people I know.

88. It is nine o'clock by my watch.

89. One must never argue from the particular to the general.

90. It's never too late to learn.

91. Which way (how) do we get to it?

92. On a peine *à* le croire.

93. Je rentre. J'ai *fait acte de présence*. Ça suffit.

94. —Mettons-nous à table ! Tu as faim ?
    —Pas *trop*. J'ai eu une *journée* terrible.

95. Ainsi, tu as bien compris ? Tu attends un quart d'heure et tu t'amènes. Je file devant.

96. Vous pouvez vous vanter *de* l'avoir *échappé belle*.

97. La *rame directe* Paris-Dinard comprend un wagon-lit et une voiture mixte 1re et 2e classes.

98. Il arrive trop souvent que l'amour ne suffit plus à celles qui ont quitté les sentiers austères de la vertu. Toutes les curiosités perverses assaillent les *égarées*.

99. « En avril ne te découvre d'un fil ;
    En mai fais comme il te plaît. »

100. « Mieux vaut tard que jamais ! »

101. Je couds mal. C'est *d'ailleurs* une *besogne* que j'exècre. Gustave *se fiche de* moi quand je casse une aiguille, quand mon fil *s'emmêle*, quand *je me pique* un doigt.

102. Demain, tous trois me *laveront la tête* pour mon absence, mais *j'en serai quitte pour* travailler le soir une heure de plus.

92. One can hardly believe it.

93. I'm off home. I've put in an appearance. That's enough.

94. —Let's sit down to dinner! Are you hungry?
    —Not so very. I've had a terrible day.

95. Now, you quite understand? You wait a quarter of an hour and (then) you come along. I'm going on ahead.

96. You can boast you had a narrow escape.

97. The through portion of the Paris-Dinard train includes a *wagon-lit* and a composite 1st and 2nd class carriage.

98. It too often happens that love alone does not suffice for women who have quitted the stern paths of virtue. Every kind of perverse curiosity assails those who have wandered.

99. 'Change not a clout till *May* be out.'

100. 'Better late than never!'

101. I sew badly. Moreover it's a job I loathe. Gustave laughs at me when I break my needle, when my thread gets tangled, when I prick my finger.

102. To-morrow, all three will give me an awful wigging for my absence, but I shall get off with working an extra hour in the evening.

103. Grâce aux *tours de faveur* dans les usines, il a toujours *à sa disposition* un châssis carrossé *livrable* en trois jours.

104. Il vaut mieux se réserver et voir d'abord *comment ça va sur le dos des* camarades.

105. *Premier invité.*— Ou signe-t-on ?
Deuxième invité.— Mon cher, c'est un mariage et non un *enterrement* ! On ne signe pas !

106. —Qui trop embrasse, mal étreint.
—Oui, ma chère, et qui a trop embrassé, mal étreint aussi.

107. —À propos, est-ce que vous êtes *libre* jeudi soir ?
—Oui, pourquoi ?

108. —J'ai les B— à dîner avec les R—.
—Et, bien entendu, le jeune L—, puisque Suzanne de R—, sera là !
—Comme vous êtes *mauvaise langue*, vous !

109. —Avez-vous *de* meilleures nouvelles de votre mère ?
—Oui, je vous remercie, elle *irait* plutôt mieux.*

110. —Je t'attends demain, pour goûter *au Claridge*.

111. —Ce n'est pas la peine de *tant* se presser.

103. Thanks to 'pull' he has in the factories, he always has at his disposal a chassis with body complete, which can be delivered inside three days.

104. Better wait and see first how the others take it.

105. *First Guest.*— Where do we sign (the book)? *Second Guest.*— My dear fellow, it's a marriage, not a funeral. We don't sign!

106. —Grasp all, lose all.
    —Yes, my dear, and a man who has hugged too much makes a poor lover.

107. —By the way, are you free Thursday evening?
    —Yes, why?

108. —I've got the B—s coming to dinner, with the R—s.
    —And, of course, young L—, as Suzanne de R—, will be there!
    —What a scandalmonger you are!

109. —Have you better news of your mother?
    —Yes, thanks, *it seems she is* going on rather better.*

    * This use of the conditional mood is especially applicable where the speaker makes an announcement on the authority of some other party—and does not desire (or is unable) to confirm it.

110. I'm expecting you to-morrow, for tea at Claridge's.

111. No need for us to hurry so.

112. —On peut l'aimer *peu ou prou*, mais on le lit, ce livre.
113. Cela devient la *scie* à la mode.

114. Il revint *très avant dans* la nuit.

115. Il est *passé maître* dans ce genre.

116. Tout le monde ne peut pas employer ce *truc*-là. Il *y* faut de grands moyens.
117. Il *écrit dans les* journaux.

118. Cela tombe à merveille !

119. Je suis *assez* de l'avis de Richard.

120. Elle est furieuse *après* toi !

121. Elle *se méprend sur* mes sentiments.

122. Chaque fin de thé, chaque station métropolitaine, chaque arrêt de l'auto, sont *autant* de *prétextes à* sortir le miroir, le *bâton de rouge*, et la *houppette*.
123. Voilà la pluie qui commence à tomber *pour de bon*.
124. Au cours du dîner, il *entra dans une colère* si violente qu'il *jeta* les assiettes et les carafes *à* la figure de sa femme.
125. *Voulez-vous de moi pour* dîner ?

112. You may like it little or much, but people are reading this book.
113. That's becoming the fashionable catchword.

114. He came back very late at night.

115. He is a past master at this sort of thing.

116. Everyone can't use that dodge. It needs big resources.
117. He writes for the papers.

118. That's splendid! (Happens most opportunely, comes just at the right time.)
119. I'm rather inclined to agree with Richard.

120. She is furious with you!

121. She is mistaken as regards my feelings.

122. The end of every tea-party, every Tube station, every stop of the car, are so many excuses for getting out the mirror, the lipstick, and the powder-puff.
123. There's the rain beginning to fall in real earnest.
124. During dinner he flew into such a violent temper that he threw the plates and decanters in his wife's face.
125. Would you like me to dine with you?

126. Elle la *serra dans* la poche de son tablier, se retourna, et marcha vers la porte. C'était une *fausse sortie.* Elle revint.

127. *Il passe* trois cents trains ici par jour.*

128. *Allez prendre* une tablette de chocolat *dans* le *distributeur.*

129. Elle était chez sa couturière. L'*essayage* ne marchait point *à son gré.*

130. Je *lui saurais mauvais gré* d'en parler.

131. Regardez, je vous prie, ce *garçon de course,* qui livre de l'épicerie sur un *tri-porteur.*

132. J'ai *des larmes plein les yeux* quand je le vois.

133. La véritable distinction *consiste* non pas *à* ne rien faire comme le voisin, mais à tout faire mieux que lui.

134. Ce pauvre X— a *ramassé une tape* épouvantable. Pas une de ses anecdotes n'a plu ! C'était *un four.*

135. Ses parents possédèrent un des derniers salons où *l'*on *se piqua* de lit*t*érature.

136. Nous habitons une toute petite maison. Elle *tiendrait dans* un *carton à chapeau.*

137. Elle regarda *en coin* les sandales attachées à mes pieds nus.

138. Elle est all*ée* s'en acheter *en catimini.*

126. She stuffed it into the pocket of her apron, turned about, and walked towards the door. It was a false exit. She came back again.

127. Three hundred trains pass here every day.*

    * Note the impersonal construction—especially applicable to statements of fact.

128. Go and get a cake of chocolate from the automatic machine.

129. She was at her dressmaker's. The fitting wasn't going at all to her liking.

130. I should hate him (her) to talk about it.

131. I ask you, look at that errand-boy, delivering groceries on a motor-trike (tricycle).

132. My eyes are full of tears when I see him.

133. Real distinction consists, not in doing nothing like your neighbour does it, but in doing everything better.

134. Poor X— has had a frightful knock. Not one of his stories went down. It was a regular frost.

135. His people had one of the last of the salons where they had pretensions to (or—prided themselves on) literature.

136. We live in a tiny little house. It would fit into a bandbox.

137. She looked askance at the sandals strapped on my bare feet.

138. She went off to buy some on the sly.

139. Il était midi. Des barques noires, *tendues* de voiles brunes, passaient *à la queue leu leu*.

140. Ce n'est pas la fortune, mais ce n'est pas la dèche.

141. Je l'ai conduit à la gare, et j'ai *chialé* pendant deux mois.

142. C'est *un* petit scandale international *que* cette histoire de ménage, *qui* s'est déroul*ée* à Paris.

143. Il y eut *séparation de corps*, et la maman *eut la garde du* petit enfant.*

    * *Séparation de corps*—résultant d'un jugement, met fin à la vie en commun des époux. Les causes sont les mêmes que les causes de divorce. La séparation de corps entraîne la *séparation de biens*. La séparation de biens peut résulter soit du contrat de mariage, soit d'un jugement. Dans ce régime-ci chaque des époux conserve la propriété et l'administration de ses biens.

144. Conduisez ce monsieur *où il voudra*.

145. —Vous n'avez pas entendu que votre patron vous a dit *de* me conduire où je *voudrais*?

    —Je ne sais pas *si j'aurai* assez d'essence. Il faut que je *fasse le plein*.

146. Le chauffeur *entra* un peu vite *dans* un *camion* mal éclairé, qui sortait d'un *chemin de traverse*.

139. It was midday. Black boats, with brown sails spread, were passing one after the other.
140. It isn't a fortune, but it isn't 'stonybrokedness.'

141. I drove him to the station, and I howled crying for two months.
142. It's a regular little international scandal, this family affair, which happened in Paris.

143. There was a legal separation, and the mother got the custody of the little boy.*

    * *Séparation de corps*—the result of a legal decree, puts an end to the living-together of married people. The causes are the same as those for divorce. *Séparation de corps* involves *séparation de biens*; the latter may be the consequence of provisions in the marriage-contract, or of a legal decree, and means that each party retains the property in and power of administration over, his or her estate.

144. Drive this gentleman wherever he wants to go. (NOTE—*Future tense.*)
145. —Did you not hear your master tell you to drive me wherever I wanted to go?
    (NOTE—*Conditional mood.*)
    —I don't know whether I shall have enough petrol. I shall have to fill up.
    (NOTE—*Future tense after* 'si,' *meaning* 'whether.')
146. The chauffeur ran a bit fast into a badly-lighted lorry, that was coming out of a side-road.

147. Elle est *guindée* dans son rôle.

148. Il peut nouer maintenant à sa boutonnière le ruban rouge *décerné* par le Ministre des Beaux-Arts.

149. *En bras de chemise* je me campai dans le salon.

150. Il a pu *combiner* cette rencontre. Mais pour qu'ils puissent se rencontrer, c'est *d'un compliqué* !

151. Voyons, Lisette, c'est trop fort. Vous *faites trop de casse*, je retiendrai ça *sur* vos gages.

152. Ce disant, elle touchait le bois de *son* parapluie, pour *conjurer le sort*.

153. *Le* service des *Objets Trouvés*, Madame ? Mais, Madame, c'est à la Préfecture de Police.

154. Je *voudrais bien* que quelqu'un m'explique un peu quelque chose de ce qui se passe.

155. Autrefois on allait passer un mois à la mer, *voire* deux. Maintenant *chacun* va et vient avec *son* auto. Qui n'en a pas ?

156. Est-ce que ça t'ennuie *de* causer avec moi de choses sérieuses ?

157. Promettre et tenir sont deux.

158. Ma mère est fort *dégoûtée*. Elle n'est pas *de son temps*.

147. She is affected (stilted) in her part (theatrical).

148. Now he can tie in his buttonhole the red ribbon bestowed by the Minister of Fine Arts.

149. In my shirt-sleeves I planted myself in the drawing-room.

150. He managed to fix up this meeting. But for them to be able to meet is a horribly complicated business!

151. Come! Lisette, this is a bit too much. You break too many things. I shall stop that out of your wages.

152. So saying, she touched the wood of her umbrella, to appease the Fates.

153. The *Lost* Property Office, Madame? Why, Madame, that's at the *Préfecture de Police*.

154. I'd like very much if someone would explain a bit what is happening.

155. Formerly, one went to spend a month at the seaside, or even two. Now, everyone goes and comes in their car. Who is there who hasn't got one?

156. Does it bore you to talk with me about serious things?

157. Promises are like piecrust.

158. My mother is very fastidious. She is not modern in her ideas.

159. Elle est *formaliste*. Elle est *dégoûtée des* façons inconvenantes de nos jours.
160. *De quelle année* est ce livre ?

161. Vous seriez si gentille de me recoudre ce bouton qui a *sauté*.
162. On l'a mis en liberté provisoire, *sous caution de* 20 000 F.
163. Dans quelles conditions le renouvellement de ce *bail* peut-il être effectué ?
164. Ce n'est pas à la portée du *premier venu*.

165. —Êtes-vous abonné a *ce* magazine ?
     —Non. Je préfère l'acheter *au numéro*.

166. Il ne faut pas que je vous *accapare* trop.

167. Tant pis si ça te *chiffonne*.

168. Êtes-vous bien sûre *de* me les avoir données, ces clés ?
169. Qui, cela *a dû* se passer ainsi.

170. Deux attitudes s'offrent ; ou bien saluer et fuir, ou bien *encaisser*.
171. Je ne pouvais guère le réveiller *en pleine nuit*.
172. Son salon *regorgeait de* plantes exotiques et de fleurs rares, on aurait dit une *serre*.

159. She is a stickler for ceremony. She is disgusted with the unseemly ways of today.
160. In what year was that book published?

161. Would you be so sweet as to sew on for me this button that has come off?
162. She (he) was released on bail of 20,000 francs.
163. On what conditions can the renewal of this lease be arranged?
164. That's not in everyone's power (to do).

165. —Do you subscribe to that magazine?
     —No. I prefer to buy it as it comes out (a number at a time).
166. I mustn't monopolise you too much.

167. Sorry if it worries you.

168. Are you quite sure you gave me those keys?
169. Yes, that's what must have happened.

170. There were two things to do; bow and flee, or else put up with it.
171. I could scarcely wake him up in the very middle of the night.
172. Her drawing-room was overflowing with exotic plants and rare flowers, one might take it for a greenhouse.

173. Ne pourrions-nous pas causer d'autre chose ? *On s'est donné le mot.* Tout le monde se fait un devoir de me poser cette question.

174. Je vais *vous pousser des colles* nouvelles.

175. Je ne veux pas qu'on me *tire les vers du nez* de cette façon.

176. Il faut *s'y mettre.*

177. Il faut que nous en *prenions* tous les deux *notre parti.*

178. *Il vint une* de ses amies, qui s'ennuyait aussi.

179. J'avais, comme *il va de soi*, toutes les *préventions* contre elle.

180. Elle a déjà fait six mois *de prévention.*

181. Ils étaient au coin du feu. Ils causaient *à bâtons rompus.*

182. Il l'a destiné à Yvonne, mais je l'ai *subtilisé.*

183. Je ne sortirai que si ça *me chante.*

184. Son auto *stationnait* à la porte.

185. Marthe avait trente ans *sonnés.*

186. Neuf et sept font seize. *Mettons* six, et un *à rapporter.*

173. Couldn't we talk of something else? It's a regular conspiracy ('the word has gone round'). Everyone thinks it their bounden duty to ask me that question.

174. I'm going to ask you some new conundrums ('posers,' tricky questions).

175. I don't want to be cross-questioned in this way.

176. We'll have to see about it.

177. We shall both of us have to reconcile ourselves to it.

178. There came along one of her girl-friends, who was also bored.

179. I had, naturally, every kind of prejudice against her.

180. She has already been six months on remand.

181. They were at the fireside. They were chatting idly.

182. He meant it for Yvonne, but I sneaked it.

183. I shan't go out unless I feel like it.

184. His car was standing at the door.

185. Marthe was over 30.

186. Nine and seven are sixteen. Put down six, and one to carry.

187. Je *remontai* Saint James Street, tournai à gauche dans la voie calme et déserte de Saint James Place, passai dans le cul-de-sac *au fond*, et gagnai le Green Park par l'*échappée* si bien connue.

188. Lui ! mais il est la *fable* de Londres !

189. J'écris, oui, non parce que j'aime écrire, mais parce que ça *me rapporte*.

190. Elle *en sera pour sa courte honte*.

191. Yvonne, la bonne, brossait le salon à l'*aspirateur*.

192. Blanche, *ayez* donc *la complaisance de* me chercher une *épingle de nourrice*.

193. —Elle est imprudente. Elle a sur elle *pour un million de* pierreries et elle *étale* tout ce *clinquant* dans les boites de nuit !
    —Mince ! Tout ça c'est *du toc !*

194. Qu'*êtes-vous devenu* depuis six mois ?

195. Alors, vous voilà ! Et vous n'avez pas *prévenu !*

196. Maintenant je suis renseigné. Je connais *la double face* de la question. Je *vois clair dans* son jeu.

197. *Pile ou face ?*

198. Ça *vous va*-t-il ?

187. I went up St. James' Street, turned left into the quiet and deserted street of St. James' Place, passed into the cul-de-sac at the end, and reached Green Park through the passage that is so well known.

188. He! Why, he's the talk of London!

189. I write, yes, not because I like writing, but because it pays me.

190. She will let herself in for a snubbing.

191. Yvonne, the maid, was cleaning out the drawing-room with the vacuum-cleaner.

192. Blanche, be so good as to find me a safety-pin.

193. —She is rash. She has a million (francs) worth of precious stones on her, and she flourishes all those 'sparklers' about in night-clubs!
    —Rot! It's all false (paste, imitation)!

194. What's become of you these last six months?

195. So, here you are! And you never let me know!

196. Now I'm made aware. I know both sides of the question. I see through his little game.

197. Heads or tails? (*Face*, *n.f.*, obverse of coin, side showing the head. *Pile*, *n.f.*, reverse.)

198. Does that suit you?

199. Elle montait son poney *à poil*.

200. Il s'est engagé *de rebours* dans une *voie à sens unique*. L'agent lui a *dressé une contravention*.

201. Nul n'est *censé* ignorer la loi.

202. Il détacha un reçu d'un *carnet à souches*.

203. Je ne viens pas pour autre chose.

204. L'application du plan Stevenson* va permettre une réduction à 70 *pour cent* du *contingent* exportable de caoutchouc.

205. Ça ne *rebute* pas trop, *encore qu*'il y ait peut-être un manque de goût.

206. Emmenez Marie, je vous *rejoins*.

207. Ce n'était pas elle, mais **son** *sosie*.

208. Elle est *en cérémonie*.

209. Passionne, il *serra à bras* sa danseuse, *sans souci de* la robe qu'il *froissait*.

210. J'ai une amie qui est très *liée avec* elle.

199. She was riding her pony bareback.

200. He entered wrong way round into a one-way street. The policeman summoned him (for an infraction of the law).

201. Nobody is presumed to be ignorant of the law.

202. He tore a receipt-form from his stub pocket-book. (NOTE— *Souche*, any stub or counterfoil. The detachable portion is *le volant*, or *la feuille volante*.)

203. That's just what I've come for.

204. The application of the Stevenson plan* will allow of (*or* allow for) the reduction to 70 per cent of the exportable allowance of rubber. [* British plan of 1920-8, to stabilise price of Malay & Ceylon rubber following post-war glut.]

205. It isn't too repulsive, though perhaps there may be a lack of good taste about it.

206. Take Marie along, I'll catch you up.

207. It wasn't her, but her double.

208. She is all dressed up (as for a ceremony).

209. Ardent, he hugged his partner, regardless of her dress that he was crumpling.

210. I have a lady-friend who is very thick (intimate) with her.

211. Je vivais *d'une* petite *vie* tranquille.

212. Elle dormait *d'un sommeil* profond.

213. Je la reconnais *pour* l'avoir vue à Auteuil (*pron.* Au-toy).
214. Parlez comme s'*il ne s'était rien passe.*

215. Il a écrit le mot *en toutes lettres.*

216. Il est bien bâti, *costaud* même.

217. Le danseur fit faire le *saut périlleux* à sa danseuse.

218. Je suis trop discret *pour* l'avoir suivi.

219. Cette petite pièce *sert de débarras,* de *fourre-tout.*
220. Elle peut être ici *d'un moment à l'autre.*

221. —Que faire un dimanche, à Londres ?
—On *se le demande,* en vérité !
222. N'est-il venu personne me demander ?

223. Voilà l'étang dont le *trop-plein* alimente les *douves* du château.
224. À quoi sert-il d'être général, et célèbre, *pour qu'*un *simple soldat* ne vous reconnaisse pas ?

211. I was living a quiet little life.

212. She was sound asleep.

213. I recognize her from having seen her at Auteuil.

214. Speak as if nothing had happened.

215. He spelled the word out in full.

216. He is strongly built, 'beefy' even.

217. The dancer made his partner turn a somersault. (NOTE— *Un saut périlleux en arrière* : a back-somersault.)

218. I *was* too discreet *to follow* him.

219. This little room serves as a lumber-room, a cubbyhole.

220. She may be here at any moment.

221. —What is one to do on a Sunday, in London?
    —You may very well ask!

222. Did nobody call to see me?

223. There is the pond whose overflow feeds the moats of the castle.

224. What's the use of being a general, and celebrated, if a private soldier doesn't recognize you?

225. J'aurais *tant voulu* voir la fin de ce film.

226. Il tient à se défaire de son *piano droit*. Il préfère l'instrument *à queue*.

227. Le condamné *s'est pourvu en cassation*.

228. Il regagna sa place, *les bras ballants*, refusé.

229. Je *dirais volontiers* qu'il est un goujat !

230. Ce n'est pas *gai gai*, mais c'est très instructif.

231. Il ira, *qu'il le veuille ou non*.

232. Il *pioche dans* son roman, dont le titre n'est pas encore *arrêté*.

233. Elle est toujours *agaçante*, *peu ou prou*.

234. Je n'*en* suis pas responsable. C'est vous qui l'avez permis ; *ne vous en prenez qu'à vous*.

235. Ensuite, tout a été *de mal en pis*.

236. —N'avez-vous pas dit qu'on l'*éconduise ?*

—*Si fait !*

225. I should so much have liked to see the end of that film.
226. He wants to get rid of his upright piano. He prefers a grand.
227. The condemned man has appealed (to the *Cour de Cassation*).
228. He returned to his seat, despondent, having been 'turned down.'
229. I'd go so far as to say he is a dirty cad!

230. It isn't very lively, but it's very instructive.

231. He'll go, whether he wants to or not.

232. He is working hard at his novel, of which the title is not yet fixed (decided).
233. She is always more or less provoking.

234. I'm not responsible for it. It was you who allowed it; don't blame anyone but yourself.
235. Afterwards, everything went from bad to worse.
236. —Didn't you say he was to be shown out (shown the door)?
    —Quite right (I did)!

Un (une) turfiste, un parieur, un bookmaker.
— A racegoer, a punter, a bookmaker.

PART VII

AT THE RACES,
POLICE & FIRE BRIGADE
& MOTORING (of 1927)

Aux courses,
Police & Pompiers
& L'Automobilisme (de 1927)

I F YOU'RE AT ALL CAREFUL, you won't get
involved with the Police. If you're at all lucky
you won't trouble the Fire Brigade. (But it's just
as well to know something about them.) And,
being Bright Young People, you will certainly
handle a car, and go to the Races. Here you will
find something about these matters.

AUX COURSES

—*Avez-vous* quelque chose?

—Je crois que *Charlot* a *toutes les chances* de gagner.

—J'ai *déniché* un joli *coup de deux* ; un vingt contre un *sur* un dix contre un.

—Tu as *fait* quelque chose?

—Oui, dans la troisième, pour les *trois ans*, cette jument de Victor. Il n'y a rien pour la battre.

—Tu aurais dû me dire que tu avais un *tuyau !*

—*J'y suis* pour mille francs *gagnant* et mille francs *placé*.

—On a fait un *essai sur* deux mille mètres. Elle est *en pleine forme*, splendide de condition, elle est imbattable.

—Le poulain de Rolland a *manqué le départ !*

—Tiens ! C'est un *faux départ !* On a cassé les *rubans !*

—En effet, ta jument *emmène* le *peloton bon train !*

—Mais, c'est la *pouliche* de Bernard qui tient la corde ! C'est un walk-over pour elle !

(En un mot comme en cent, *Charlot* finit le dernier ; la jument de Victor s'assit dans l'herbe, la pouliche de Bernard resta *dans les choux*.

AT THE RACES

—Do you know anything (have you anything good)?

—I think *Charlot* has every chance of winning.

—I've unearthed a nice double; a 20-to-1 and a 10-to-1.

—Have you backed anything?

—Yes, in the third (race), for 3-year-olds, that mare of Victor's. There's nothing to beat her.

—You might have told me you had a tip!

—I'm on for 1,000 francs to win and 1,000 francs for a place.

—They've had a trial over 2,000 metres. She is in top form, and splendid condition, she can't be beaten.

—Rolland's colt has been left at the post!

—Hold on! It's a false start! They've broken the tapes!

—Indeed, your mare is leading the field at a fine pace!

—But that filly of Bernard's has got on the rails! It's a walk-over for her!

(To cut a long story short, *Charlot* finished last; Victor's mare 'sat in the grass,' Bernard's filly was down the course (in the cabbage-

C'est un cent contre un, *de derrière les fagots*, qui a gagné. C'est moi, moi qui parle, qui n'avait point de tuyau, qui n'a rien dit et rien su, qui vient de toucher le gagnant. Viens faire un tour au *pesage* avant de rentrer aux *tribunes*.)

Résultats et rapports officiels

Prix de A—. 12 000 F. 2 000 mètres.

1. *Kipper*, à M. Dupont (E. Chantecler).
2. *Bloater*.
3. *Herring*.

Non placés—Ette, Cette, Aira, etc.
8 partants, 2 long., Courte tête. Encol.

Pesage : G. 105 F ; *pl.* 60 F ; 85 F ; 40 F.
Pelouse : G. 75 F ; *pl.* 50 F ; 40 F ; 30 F.

(Tout cela n'est qu'un rêve, naturellement !)

patch). It was a 100 to 1 chance, a rank outsider (from behind the sticks), that won. And it is I —I who speak, who had no tip whatever, and who said nothing and knew nothing, that have backed the winner. Come and take a turn in the paddock before going back to the stands.)

Results and Official Returns

A—Stakes. 12,000 francs; 2,000 metres.

1st *Kipper.* Owner, M. Dupont,
            Jockey, E. Chantecler.
2nd *Bloater.*
3rd *Herring.*
Also ran—*Ette, Cette, Aira,* etc. 8 starters.
Won by 2 lengths; *Bloater* was a short head in front of *Herring,* and *Herring* was a neck in front of the fourth horse.
The pari-mutuel paid:
In the Paddock—*Winner,* 105 to 1;
    Placed horses (1) 60/1, (2) 85/1, (3) 40/1.
On the Lawns—*Winner,* 75 to 1;
    Placed horses (1) 50/1, (2) 40/1, (3) 30/1.

(All this is but a dream—of course!)

Les Secrets d'écurie

Mademoiselle Marthe, de la Comédie-Française, est une jeune femme qui veut « *en être* ».

Elle vient *de se faire acheter* un cheval de course.

Elle *ignore tout du* cheval.

Monsieur A— est l'entraîneur de la nouvelle propriétaire.

Monsieur A— *conseille à* Mlle Marthe de réserver la bête pour une « *fin de saison* ».

Mlle Marthe, qui veut *épater* ses petites amies, insiste que « son cheval » *coure* tous les dimanches !

Monsieur A—, qui sait très bien qu'il *ne peut rien contre* Mlle Marthe, fait une *épreuve* discrète. Il dissimule ses sentiments.

Le dimanche, « son cheval » *prit le départ*, sans trop de façons, et suit le *peloton*.

« C'est une vache ! dit Monsieur A—.

—Attendez ! » dit Mlle Marthe.

Le dimanche prochain, il *recourt*.

Son jockey, obéissant aux ordres de Monsieur A—, fait une *course d'attente*. Il finit le dernier.

Le dimanche prochain, c'est Mlle Marthe qui, donne les ordres. Elle ordonne « Vous *prenez la tête* au départ et vous la gardez ! »

De *mémoire de* sportsman on ne vit jamais *pareille course.*

STABLE SECRETS

Mademoiselle Marthe, of the Comédie-Française, is a young woman who wants to be 'in the swim.'

She has just had a racehorse bought for her.

She knows nothing whatever about a horse.

Monsieur A— is trainer for the new owner.

Monsieur A— advises Mlle Marthe to keep the beast over for something 'in the back-end.' Mlle Marthe, who wants to astonish her little girl-friends, insists that 'her horse' shall run every Sunday!

Monsieur A—, who knows quite well that he cannot stand up to Mlle Marthe, has a discreet trial. He hides his feelings.

On Sunday, 'her horse' went to the post, without too much fuss, and followed the field home.

'It's a cow!' says Monsieur A—.

'You wait!' says Mlle Marthe.

Next Sunday, he runs again.

His jockey, obeying Monsieur A—'s orders, rides a waiting race. He finishes last.

The Sunday after, 'tis Mlle Marthe who gives the orders. 'You get off in front,' she ordains, 'and you stay there!'

Never was such a race seen in the memory of any sportsman.

Cravaché du départ à l'arrivée, son cheval *fuit devant lui !* Il entre dans la *ligne droite*, tout le peloton *allongé* derrière lui. Il passe le *poteau*, et finit *loin devant*.

Mlle Marthe, qui se précipite pour le conduire elle-même aux *balances*, est accueillie par les parieurs qui vocifèrent.

Ces parieurs ont, du sport, une idée qui n'est pas la bonne.

Les commissaires *demandent* quelques *explications* à Monsieur A—. Vous savez *comme sont* les commissaires.

La sonnette *tinte*, le *rouge* est mis, et sur le *tableau* on lit '2 300 F' !

Le cheval de Mlle Marthe a *trouvé moyen* de gagner son avoine.

Mais, comme la casaque orange n'est plus très populaire *auprès des* foules, Mlle Marthe va *liquider* son écurie.

(Note— *The above is an example of the use of the historical present tense in narration. The idea is that the hearer is made, as it were, an eye-witness of the events described, and a more dramatic turn is given to the recital.*)

Flogged from start to finish, 'her horse' fairly runs away from himself! He comes into the straight, all the field strung out behind him. He passes the winning-post, finishing far in front.

Mlle Marthe, who flies to lead him in herself to scale, is greeted by the howling punters.

These punters have quite wrong ideas about sport.

The stewards ask Monsieur A— for some explanations. You know what stewards are like.

The bell rings, the red ('all right') is hoisted, and on the indicator board we read '2,300 francs' (to 1).

Mlle Marthe's horse has found a way to earn his oats.

But, as the orange jacket is no longer very popular with the crowd, Mlle Marthe is selling off her stable.

⚜

LA BELLE MARTINGALE

C'est sur l'hippodrome de Saint-Cloud, le 6 juin 1927, que le célèbre Père La Cerise a réalisé la merveilleuse aventure qu'il a raconté ainsi qu'il suit :

« Je suis arrivé *clochard* ou à peu près, puisque j'avais deux *thunes*. Dans les deux premières je *reste peinard*. Dans le prix de Début je *colle ma fortune* sur Ranaï. Je touche 129 francs. Je mets 100 francs sur Fortunio dans la grande épreuve… et le reste *à gauche*… comme assurance. Je touche 810 *balles*. Ma foi, *je me risque !* J'emprunte à un copain *de quoi* faire *le sac*, et je touche dans le Velasquez ce brave Orange Pip II… c'est parce que je venais de déjeuner d'une orange, dont j'avais avalé quelques pépins par accident… Total— 19 650 francs ! Vous pensez que je ne reste pas pour la dernière ! »

(*Cette histoire est véridique.*)

Playing It Up Nicely

'Twas on the ràcecourse of Saint-Cloud, on June 6th 1927, that the celebrated 'Father Cherry' (*itinerant vendor of race cards and modest punter*) brought off the marvellous event which he has related as below:

'I was pretty well broke when I got there, for I had only ten francs. I stood off (didn't bet) in the first two races. In the *Prix de Début* I shoved the lot on Ranaï. I collected 129 francs. I put 100 of that on Fortunio in the big race … and set the rest aside as an insurance. … I collected 810 francs. My word, I went all out then! I borrowed enough from a pal to make up a 'sack' (1000 francs) … and pulled it off on good old Orange Pip II in the *Prix Velasquez* … that was because I'd just lunched off an orange and had accidentally swallowed some of the pips. … So I notched 19,650 francs! You may be sure I didn't wait for the last race!'

(*N.B.— The above is a true yarn.*)

POLICE & POMPIERS
Police-forces & Fire Brigades

1. Police duties in France are performed by the following bodies:

(a) *La Sûreté*—or Criminal Investigation Police, directly dependent upon the Central Government Administration. Its *personnel* are called *agents*, *inspecteurs*, etc., *de la Sûreté*.

(b) *La Police municipale*—or Municipal Police, dependent in Paris upon the *Préfecture de Police*, and comprising both uniformed services (*gardiens de la paix*), and a detective force. The correct term for a policeman is *agent*, *inspecteur*, etc., and he should be addressed as '*monsieur l'agent*,' '*monsieur l'inspecteur*,' etc. (It is a common error for English-speaking people to term a policeman in Paris a '*gendarme*.') The police-stations in the several *arrondissements* of Paris are termed '*commissariats de police*.'

(c) *La Gendarmerie*—a corps of Military Police dependent upon the War Office (*Ministère de la Guerre*) and concerned primarily with the enforcement of the military obligations of citizens. This force performs police duties in the country districts. The *personnel* are termed *gendarme*, *brigadier* (corporal), etc.

2. *Un commissaire de police* is a police magistrate charged with the maintenance of order within his jurisdiction. His office is *le commissariat* (*de police*).

   Un juge d'instruction is an examining magistrate, charged with the investigation of crimes and misdemeanours, with the apprehension (*arrestation*) of accused persons (*prévenus*), and the preparation of all necessary evidence. The French system of criminal procedure differs widely from that in England, the *juge d'instruction* having very wide powers. It is customary, for instance, to effect the *confrontation* of the accused with witnesses, and of witnesses with one another, in order to test their statements.

   Le Parquet is a subsidiary of the office of the Public Prosecutor (*Procureur de la République*), to which complaints may be addressed with a view to the institution of criminal proceedings.

3. In Paris the Fire Brigade is a unit of the Active Regular Army, known as the corps of '*Sapeurs-pompiers*.'
   A Fire-Alarm is *un avertisseur* (*d'incendie*).
   A Fire-Station is *un poste d'incendie*.

L'AUTOMOBILISME (DE 1927)

1. Ce moteur a 125 mm *d'alésage avec* 150 mm de course.
2. Le moteur *donne* mal ; il y a des *ratés*.

3. Cette valve *fuit*.
4. J'ai senti la voiture *déraper*.
5. *Passez en troisième*.
6. La voiture *démarrait* doucement.
7. Une bougie *s'encrassait*.
8. Il faut *déboucher* le *gicleur*.
9. Nous avons *éclaté* un pneu.
10. *Vidanger* le *carter* tous les 1 500 km est suffisant pour presque tous les moteurs. *Refaire le plein* avec l'huile fraîche.
11. Faut bien enduire *de dissolution* la face de la *pastille*.
12. J'étais *en panne* (*en rade*, *en carafe*) sur la route de N—.
13. Mettez-moi en marche, mes « *accus* » sont *à plat*.
14. Le *réglage* d'un moteur est une question d'oreille.
15. Nous nous installâmes dans ma conduite intérieure, et « fouette cocher ! » en route !
16. Je conduis depuis cinq ans et *jamais il ne m'est arrivé d'accident !* Touche du bois !
17. Il faut des manœuvres assez précises pour entrer dans ce garage *en marche arrière*.

MOTORING (OF 1927)

1. This engine has a bore of 125 mm and a stroke of 150 mm.
2. The engine is running (firing) badly; there are misfires.
3. This valve is leaking.
4. I felt the car skid.
5. Change into third (gear).
6. The car started off smoothly.
7. A sparking-plug (spark plug) sooted up.
8. You must clean out the jet.
9. We've burst a tyre.
10. Emptying the crank-chamber every 1,500 km is enough with almost all engines. Fill up again with fresh oil.
11. You must smear the face of the patch well with solution.
12. I had a breakdown on the N— road.

13. Give me a wind-up (a crank up), my accumulators have run down.
14. Tuning an engine is a matter of ear.
15. We tucked ourselves into my saloon, and, 'touch-'em-up, coachman!'—off we went!
16. I've been driving for five years, and never had an accident happen me! Touch wood!
17. It wants some rather nice manœuvring to back into this garage.

18. Les voitures américaines sont très *démulti-pliées*. Leur conduite est donc très agréable, mais cet agrément *se paie* par une *consom-mation* d'essence assez élevée.

19. Tout ça *sent* l'essence !

DANS QUELLES CONDITIONS PEUT-IL ARRIVER QU'UN MOTEUR SE METTE À COGNER ?

1° Les *dépôts* de charbon *provenant des* combustions incomplètes et de la décomposition des huiles de graissage, *tout en* réduisant *le* volume des chambres, peuvent rester en ignition après l'explosion et *provoquer* des allumages prématurés.

[Ce *cognage* par encrassement est un *martellement* sourd, localisé dans la tête des cylindres. On le *décèle en côte*, aux *reprises*, pendant les accélérations *en palier*.

On a l'impression que le moteur ne tourne pas librement et qu'il retient la voiture. Ceci se produit quand le moteur est chaud ; *lors des* départs, et l'eau étant froide, la *marche* paraît normale.

Il est alors indispensable de procéder à la décarbonisation.]

2° Il y a aussi le cognage provenant de l'*usure* des coussinets ou des têtes des bielles.

18. American cars are geared very low. They are therefore very pleasant to drive, but this advantage is paid for by rather a high petrol consumption.
19. The whole thing smells of petrol!

What Makes an Engine Start Knocking?

1. Carbon deposits arising from incomplete combustion and from the decomposition of lubricating oils, whilst reducing the volume of the combustion chambers, may remain burning after the explosion and cause premature ignitions.

   [This (kind of) knocking due to sooting-up is a dull hammering, localised in the cylinder-heads. It is found (when running) up-hill, when picking-up, and when accelerating in top gear.

   One gets the impression that the engine is not turning (over) freely, and that it is holding the car back. This happens when the engine is hot; when starting off, and with the water cold, the running seems normal.

   It is then essential to go in for decarbonisation.]

2. There is also a knocking arising from wear of bearings or big ends.

[Ce cognage a *un* caractère métallique, c'est le choc entre les pièces qui ont du *jeu* dans leur assemblage, et l'on le distingue particulièrement en *emballant* le moteur *à vide*.]

3° Il y a aussi le cognage du *cliquetis* par excès *d'avance* à l'allumage.

[Ce dernier se perçoit surtout en côte, ou dans un passage difficile où le moteur *tire* durement.]

Routes françaises et système de kilométrage, Classification des routes [1927]

1. Les routes nationales. (R.N.)
2. Les routes départementales. (R.D.)
3. Les chemins de grande communication. (Ch. de G^{de} C^{on} *ou* C.G.C.)
4. Les chemins d'intérêt commun. (C.I.C.)
5. Les chemins vicinaux.

Le kilométrage est indiqué par les *bornes kilométriques et plaques indicatrices* des Ponts et Chaussées.

Les routes nationales, et la plupart des routes départementales, chemins de G.C., ou d'intérêt commun, portent sur leurs bornes ou plaques (dont les formes sont particulières) un *numéro administratif*, servant à les distinguer par toute leur étendue.

[This knocking has a metallic character, being the shock between parts which have play in their fitting, and it is especially noticeable when racing the engine without load.]

3. There is also the rattling (kind of) knocking, from excessive advance of the ignition.

[This latter is especially noticed (when running) up-hill or during some difficult bit of running, when the engine is pulling hard.]

FRENCH ROADS AND ROAD-SIGNS, CLASSIFICATION OF ROADS [1927]

1. National Roads.
2. Departmental Roads.
3. Highways.
4. Third-class Roads.
5. By-roads.

Kilometrage [road-distance(s)] is shown by the kilomètre-posts and direction-plates of the *Ponts et Chaussées* (*the Government Department, of the Ministry of Public Works, responsible for construction and maintenance*).

The National Roads, and the majority of Departmental Roads, Highways, and Third-Class Roads, bear on their posts (whose shapes are distinctive) an 'administrative number,' serving to distinguish them throughout their length.

En général, les bornes présentent trois faces. Sur la face centrale on lit la désignation abrégée (R.N. etc.) suivie du numéro administratif, et d'un chiffre kilométrique indiquant la distance de l'origine du kilométrage. (Cette origine est, le plus souvent, inconnue *du* touriste.)

Sur les faces latérales on lit le nom et la distance de la ville etc. vers laquelle on se dirige.

Les plaques indicatrices portent également ces indications.

Donc, rien n'est plus facile que de vérifier si la route suivie est *la bonne*.

Les Signaux de route

Les signaux de route, placés sur des poteaux à droite de la route et quelques 250 mètres avant l'obstacle, indiquent : les *cassis ;* les *virages ;* les *croisements ;* et les *passages à niveau.*

Le Code de la route

Le code de la route [*de 1922*] est modifié (avril 1927) pour donner de la priorité en faveur *du* véhicule qui vient à droite. (Naturellement, en France, on *conduit* en tenant à droite, au rebours du code anglais, etc.)

Generally speaking, the posts show three faces. On the central face one reads the abbreviated designation (R.N. etc.), followed by the 'administrative number,' and a kilometre figure indicating the distance from the starting-point of the measurement. (This starting-point will, more often than not, be unknown to the tourist.)

On the lateral faces one reads the name and distance of the town, etc., towards which one is travelling.

The Direction Plates likewise bear these indications.

So nothing is easier than to verify whether the road followed is the right one or not.

Road Warnings

Road warnings, placed on posts to the right of the road and some 250 metres before the obstacles, indicate: *open drains*, *bends*, *cross-roads*, and *level-crossings*.

The Rule(s) of the Road

The [*1922*] rule of the road has been changed (April 1927) so as to give priority to a vehicle approaching on one's right-hand side (*i.e.* at road junctions). Naturally, in France, you keep to the right when driving, contrary to the English (etc.) rule.

PART VIII

STILL MORE TABLE TALK
—Et autres propos de table

236 more idiomatic sentences
236 phrases idiomatiques supplémentaires

S TILL MORE 'TABLE TALK.' —Again, you can open it anywhere, and learn something.

—ET AUTRES PROPOS DE TABLE

1. Quand on a perdu l'amour on ne fait plus que se survivre.
2. On fait contre mauvaise fortune bon cœur.

3. Regarde ! C'est la fille du patron qui a *réussi*.
4. —Comment la trouvez-vous ?
   —Quelconque.

5. Elle veut le marier *avec* cette jeune fille.

6. *Que* la Jeannette d'autrefois me paraît être éloignée de la jeune femme *que me voilà devenue. Que d'*illusions envolées ! *Pauvre de moi !*
7. Bon ! Vous allez voir *de quel bois je me chauffe !*
8. Je ne vous reconnais pas. Vous *prenez l'accent* américain !
9. Nous nous sommes très bien *débrouillés* sans eux.
10. Je ne parie pas. Il n'est pas amusant de gagner *à coup sûr*.
11. Personne n'y trouve *à redire*.

12. Nous pourrions rentrer. *Il va être* l'heure du thé.

STILL MORE TABLE TALK

1. When love is lost one is merely outliving oneself.

2. One must bear up against ill-fortune.

3. Look! There's the boss's daughter. She's got on all right.

4. —What do you think of her?
   —Not much.
   (NOTE— Not *quelleconque* in fem.)

5. She wants to marry him *to* that girl.

6. How far away the Jeannette of once-upon-a-time seems from the young woman I've become! How many illusions flown! Poor me!

7. Right! You shall see the sort of stuff I'm made of.

8. I can't recognize you. You're cultivating an American accent!

9. We got on very well without them.

10. I'm not betting. It isn't amusing to bet on certainties.

11. Nobody finds any fault with it (raises any objections).

12. We should go back to the house. It's near tea-time.

13. Je l'ai toujours su, *alors même que* je n'étais qu'une petite fille.
14. Je l'ai vu *boire à* (*même*) la bouteille.*

15. Il a *mangé à même* le plat.*

16. Il se couchait *à même* le tapis.

17. Que de fois je me suis étendu *à même ces planches* humides !
18. Nous nous sommes laissés aller *au fil de l'eau*.
19. Ces allumettes *coûtent* joliment *cher*, mais elles ne *prennent* pas.
20. —Il ne t'a jamais rien dit de moi ?
    —Non, rien.
    —J'*aime autant* ; d'ailleurs tu n'aurais pas compris *non plus*.
21. Je ne *vous savais* pas ici.

22. A-t-il été recalé à son examen ?

23. Elle a *trop présumé de* ses forces.

24. Elles sont impayables, ces deux sœurs ! Elles *jacassent* comme *des réveille-matin(s) arrivés à terme* !

25. C'est du sport *et du bon*.

13. I always knew it, even when I was only a small girl.

14. I saw him drinking out of (straight from) the bottle.*

15. He ate off the plate.*

* *Literally*—to drink *out of* a bottle, eat *off* a plate, etc., is boire *dans* une bouteille, manger *dans* un plat.

16. He lay down on the bare carpet.

17. How many times have I stretched myself out on these *bare* wet planks!

18. We let ourselves drift with the current.

19. These matches cost a jolly lot, but they won't strike.

20. —He didn't ever say anything to you about me? —No, nothing. —I'm just as glad. Besides, you wouldn't have understood, either.

21. I didn't know you were here.

22. Has he been 'spun' again for (failed to pass) his examination?

23. She has over-rated her strength.

24. They're priceless, those two sisters! They chatter like alarm-clocks going off! (NOTE—*'Réveille-matin'*, *masc.*; abbrev. *'réveil'*; pl.: *formerly invar., now also '- -s'.*)

25. It is sport, and good sport too!

26. Le boxeur était un jeune garçon brun à la figure *étonnée*.

27. Voyons, ma petite, *tu es* bien *de ton village !* Tache seulement de ne pas faire cette mine *niaise*.

28. Le déjeuner était *pour* une heure. Nous arrivons à une heure et demie.
    « *On ne vous espérait plus* » fait Madame.

29. Elle n'entend ni à *hue* ni à *dia*.*

30. Elle tire *à hue et à dia*.*

31. *Il est des* vertus insolentes que faire trébucher est non seulement un plaisir *mais encore* un devoir.

32. Son écriture se rapproche de l'hiéroglyphe plus que du *jambage*.

33. Elle n'en a *déparlé* pendant quinze jours.

34. *Accouche*, vieux ! On sonne la fin de l'entr'acte.

35. —Mais, man cher, tu deviens *maboul !*
    —Nenni-dà ! C'est toi qui es *marteau !*

36. Nous ne prendrons que la moindre chose *sur le pouce*, avant le théâtre.

37. J'ai gardé le taxi. Puis-je vous *pousser un bout ?*

38. Vous allez *prendre la clef des champs ?*

26. The boxer was a dark young boy with a wrinkled face.

27. Come, little girl! You are indeed just up from the country! Just try not to look such a simpleton.

28. Luncheon was at one. We arrived at half-past one.
    'We had given you up,' said Madame.

29. She won't listen to any reason.

30. She won't make up her mind (won't settle to anything). [* NOTE— *Hue !* Right! & *Dia !* Left! —Ejaculations by which a carman or ploughman guides his horses, (*cf.* English 'Haw!' & 'Gee!')]

31. There are some virtues so arrogant that to trip them up is not only a pleasure, but rather a duty.

32. His (her) writing is more like hieroglyphics than script.

33. She never stopped talking about it for a fortnight.

34. Out with it, old man! There's the bell for the end of the interval.

35. —But, my dear fellow, you're going crazy! —Not at all! It's you who're a bit mad!

36. We're only having a pick at something (a 'snack') before the theatre.

37. I've kept the taxi. Can I give you a lift?

38. You're going to clear off?

39.   La situation est on *ne peut plus calme.*

40.   Maintenant je vais vous mettre au courant de votre *boulot.*

41.   Il se *retint à quatre pour* ne pas *s'esclaffer.*

42.   Il s'est *mis en quatre pour* eux.

43.   Oui, je l'ai vu passer. Elle était *tirée à quatre épingles !*

44.   J'ai une faim de loup. Je vais *manger pour quatre !*

45.   Pour cette *épreuve* la *monte à califourchon* est interdite. Il faut monter *en amazone.*

46.   Ils avaient vingt-cinq ans, *à deux mois l'un de l'autre.*

47.   « Je t'*y prends !* » cria-t-elle.

48.   Pour ne pas *être en reste de* politesse *avec* lui, je l'invitai à déjeuner.

49.   Qu'avez-vous *à* me regarder comme ça ?

50.   Bien sûr. Ça passera comme une lettre à la poste.

51.   Il a *sauté sur l'aubaine.*

52.   Comment s'appelle-t-elle déjà *de son petit nom ?*

53.   Madame, je vous *présente* mon ami, *le* professeur Y—.

39. The situation couldn't be calmer.

40. Now I'm going to post you up (bring you up to date) in your job.

41. He did his level best not to burst out laughing.

42. He did his level best for them.

43. Yes, I saw her pass by. She was togged up to the nines!

44. I'm as hungry as a wolf. I'm going to eat enough for four!

45. In this event (competition) riding astride is barred. You must ride side-saddle.

46. They were 25, with two months between them.

47. 'I've caught you in the act!' she cried.

48. So as not to be behindhand with him in politeness, I asked him to lunch.

49. What's up with you, looking at me like that?

50. Sure thing! It will be as easy as shelling peas.

51. He jumped at the chance.

52. What on earth is her Christian name (first name)?

53. Madame, let me introduce my friend Professor Y—.

54. Cette année le Mardi gras *tombe un* treize.

55. Eh bien ! Tu as *fait du propre !*

56. …La *place* me manque pour vous *parler* aujourd'hui des S—.
(Notez bien que cette phrase a été écrite.)

57. Il y avait dans la voix *un rien de* jalousie.

58. Il y avait une foule ; on *refusait du monde.*

59. *De* savants psychologues *sont parvenus à* isoler *le* bacille de l'amour. Il a la forme d'un point d'interrogation.

60. Je vais *faire d'une pierre deux coups.*

61. Elle contemplait *l'un* de ses bas, *où* quelques *mailles* étaient rompues.

62. *Sur le moment*, je ne devinai pas ce qui *me valait* cette faveur.

63. Elle *veut rien savoir.*

64. *Si* Mademoiselle veut que j'*aille* avec elle ?

65. Cette porte *donne* sur le perron.

66. Cette fenêtre *donne* sur *la* cour.

54. This year Shrove Tuesday falls on the 13th.

55. Well! You've made a nice mess of things!

56. ... I've no room to tell you to-day about the Smiths. [See p. 268].
    (NOTE—This phrase was *written*.)

57. There was a tinge of jealousy in the voice.

58. There was a crowd, they were turning people away.

59. Learned psychologists have managed to isolate the bacillus of love. It is shaped like a note of interrogation (question mark).

60. I'm going to kill two birds with one stone.

61. She was contemplating one of her stockings, where some of the threads were broken.

62. At the time I didn't guess to what it was I owed this favour.

63. She won't have it (won't entertain it).

64. Perhaps Mademoiselle would like me to go with her?
    (In this impersonal construction, the question might be addressed to a third party, or to Mlle herself.)

65. This door opens on to the steps.
    (NOTE—*Un perron* is always outdoor. An internal stairway is *un escalier*.)

66. This window looks out on the courtyard.

67. Son navire a *donné* sur un écueil.

68. Le soleil *donnait* dans la chambre.

69. Il *donnait de la tête* contre un mur.

70. L'eau sera bientôt *amenée dans* la maison.

71. Il ne faut pas *juger* les gens *sur l'apparence.*

72. Ce *legs* (*pron. lè*) ne fut pas très *goûté* par les héritiers.

73. Elle a accepté une *transaction.*

74. *Heureusement que* j'ai du soin, et que mes robes peuvent encore *tenir le coup,* mais ça ne *saurait* durer.

75. *De son vrai nom* elle s'appelait M—. Elle *chantait faux.*

76. Je viens de lui donner *ses huit jours.*

77. —Où est *donc* la petite Claudine ?

78. —La voilà, jambes allongées, dans *un transatlantique.*

79. J'ai *fait fixer à* mon auto *un* porte-bagages qui supportera très bien trois valises *en vache.*

80. Il croquait un *pied* de céleri.

67. His ship has struck a reef (rock).
    (NOTE—*Un écueil* is always submerged or partly so. *Un rocher* is a high rock.)
68. The sun was shining into the room.

69. He ran his head against a wall.

70. Water will soon be laid on to the house.

71. You mustn't judge people by appearances.

72. This legacy wasn't much to the liking of the heirs.
73. She has agreed to a compromise.

74. Luckily I'm careful, and my dresses are still presentable, but this sort of thing can't go on.
75. Her real name was M—. She used to sing out of tune.
76. I've just given him (her) a week's notice.

77. —Where has little Claudine got to?

78. —There she is, legs stretched out, in a deck-chair.
79. I've had a luggage-carrier fixed on my car, which will easily take three leather trunks.

80. He was munching a stick of celery.

81. Les critiques le *prenaient* fort *au sérieux*.

82. Elle est simplement soucieuse de *ménager la chèvre et le chou*.

83. Vous *direz* à la femme de chambre *de mettre* les *embauchoirs* dans mes souliers.

84. C'est tout ce que tu as *comme* bagage ?

85. Il doit être assez agréable d'*avoir* de l'argent *à n'en savoir que faire*.

86. *Du jour au lendemain* il s'est fait un nom.

87. C'est gentil *de sa part*.

88. —Alors, c'est bon ?
    —*C'est selon.*

89. *Par surcroît*, il a une veine de pendu !

90. *Pour un* été chaud, on peut dire que nous avons un été chaud !

91. Il paraît à son aise *à peu près comme* un poisson sur de la paille.

92. Je ne sais vraiment *comment* vous remercier.

93. Elle en a *une peur bleue*. Vous n'avez pas idée de ce qu'il peut se montrer *buté*, lorsqu'une fois *il s'est fourré* quelque chose dans la tête.

94. Il tira de son portefeuille une belle *coupure* de mille francs.

81. The critics took him very seriously.

82. She merely wants to run with the hare and hunt with the hounds.

83. Kindly tell the maid to put the trees in my shoes.

84. Is that all you have in the way of baggage?

85. It must be rather nice to have so much money you don't know what to do with it.

86. He made a name for himself in a day.

87. That's very nice of him (her).

88. —So that's all right?
    —It all depends (that's as may be).

89. Moreover, he has the devil's own luck!

90. You may jolly well say we are having a hot summer!

91. He seems about as comfortable as a fish out of water.

92. I really don't know how to thank you.

93. She is in a blue funk of him. (*—colloquial*)
    You've no idea how stubborn he can be, once he's got something into his head.

94. He drew a fine 1000-franc note from his pocket-book.

95. Oh ! Montrez-le-moi, mon cher ; *c'est que* je n'en ai jamais vu, vous savez !

96. Pour réussir, il faut avoir de l'assurance, un certain *toupet*. La timidité n'est pas du tout votre *fait*.

97. Je suis devenu tant soit peu conn*ai*sseur.

98. Moi je suis campagnard, peu accoutumé aux *veilles*.

99. C'est joliment de la chance qu'il n'y *eût* personne là !

100. Monsieur et Madame Un Tel se sont embarqués pour un voyage *en* Chine et *aux* Indes. Ils espèrent *être de retour* à Paris pour Noël. On ne *fera pas suivre* le courrier.

101. C'est elle qui fait marcher la maison, qui mène les domestiques, qui donne les ordres.

102. Il est le premier chi*rurg*ien *de* Londres.

103. Pour l'instant, elle est installée rue d'Astorg, en attendant *la crémaillère** du petit hôtel qu'elle est *en train de* se faire construire à Neuilly.

    * *Crémaillère— Lit.* Pot-hook, hanger, from which cooking-pots used to hang. *'Pendre la —.'* (*fam.*) : To give a house-warming party.

104. J'avoue que je ne suis pas extrêmement *chaud*.

105. Il faut voir les choses *telles qu'elles sont*.

95. Oh! show it me, my dear, do you know I've never seen one!

96. To succeed, you must have assurance, a bit of cheek. Shyness is not at all what you want.

97. I've become a bit of a conn*oi*sseur. (Note the difference in spelling.)

98. I'm a country bumpkin, not used to late nights.

99. Jolly lucky nobody was there!

100. Monsieur and Madame So-and-so have sailed for a trip to China and India. They hope to be back in Paris for Christmas. Letters will not be forwarded.

101. 'Tis she who runs the house, looks after the servants, and gives the orders.

102. He is the leading surgeon in London.

103. For the moment she is living in the Rue d'Astorg pending completion of the little house (mansion) she is having built for herself at Neuilly.

104. I confess I'm not very keen (about it).

105. One must look facts in the face.

106. Je commence à *en avoir assez*, de ses façons.
107. Je n'ai pas la moindre intention d'*en démordre*.
108. Maintenant vous devez pouvoir voyager *tout votre content*.
109. Cet endroit nous déplaît *au dernier point*.

110. Je demeure *du côté de* la place Clichy.

111. Quant à la famille, il y a une sœur *montée en graine…*
112. S'ils étaient tous *ainsi* nous n'*aurions* pas *à* nous plaindre.
113. Je vous verrai ce soir, vous me direz comment ça *se sera passé avec* votre amie.
114. —Vous l'avez *mis au courant* ?
—Non.
—Vous auriez pu *pendant que vous y étiez*.

115. Tout ça *c'est la bouteille à l'encre*.

116. Elle sait se mettre *à la hauteur* de toutes les situations.
117. Et vous, Madame, vous *adonnez*-vous aussi *au* bridge ?
118. —Alors, Madame, vous ne jouez pas au bridge ?
— Non. *Tout ce qui est* jeu m'ennuie.
119. Le patron vient de le *remercier*.

106. I'm beginning to be a bit fed up with her goings-on.
107. I haven't the least intention of going back on it.
108. Now you ought to be able to travel as much as you like.
109. This place is utterly detestable to us.

110. I live over near the Place Clichy.

111. As for the family, there's a sister who's an old maid ...
112. If they were all like that, we shouldn't need to grumble.
113. I'll see you this evening (and) you'll tell me how things went with your friend.
114. —Did you tell him about it?
    —No.
    —You might as well have, while you were about it.
115. The whole thing is a mystery.

116. She knows the right thing to do in any circumstances.
117. And do you go in for bridge, too, Madame?
118. —So, Madame, you do not play bridge?
    —No. Everything in the way of games bores me.
119. The boss has just given him the sack.

120. Il serait bien *difficile de* se décider dans la vie, lorsqu'on a l'embarras *du* choix, si l'on ne possédait la suprême ressource de *tirer à la courte paille*.

121. C'est le fils d'un grand souverain. Il *s'en fallut de peu* qu'il ne régnât.

122. Elle *assistait à* une divertissante *parade foraine*, où elle s'amusait, ou du moins *faisait semblant*, ce qui est *tout comme*.

123. N'est-ce point lui qui disait le plus sérieusement du monde : « Non, l'automobile, ça ne *prendra* pas, c'est une invention *mort-née !* Nous reviendrons aux chevaux… » ?

124. En ce qui concerne l'amour, je déteste les gens de gros appétit. *De temps à autre* savourer un repas fin, *soit*. Mais plutôt ne jamais manger *que de* s'asseoir au réfectoire commun devant une *platée* vulgaire.

125. —Comment va-t-il ?
    —Il est *au plus mal*, il est *perdu*, ce n'est plus qu'une question d'heures.

126. Elle est méfiante *de sa nature*.

127. J'en ai *plein le dos*.

128. Ça venait comme des cheveux sur la soupe, tout à fait déplacé.

120. It would be very hard to make up one's mind in life, when one has too many alternatives, did one not enjoy the last resource of drawing lots.

121. That's the son of a great Sovereign. He was very near coming to the throne.

122. She was watching an entertaining show at the fair, where she was amusing herself, or at least pretending to do so, which comes to the same thing.

123. Wasn't it he who said, in the most serious way in the world, 'No! Motors! They won't catch on, they're a still-born invention! We shall go back to horses…'?

124. In matters relating to love, I loathe people of gross appetite. To enjoy a delicate meal now and then, why, all well and good. But better never to eat at all than to sit down in the common-room to a vulgar heaped plateful.

125. —How is he going on?
     —He's as bad as he can be, he's done for, it's only a matter of hours now.

126. She is distrustful by nature.

127. I'm fed up with it.

128. That happened like hairs in the soup, quite out of place.

129. Je ne sais plus *de quel bois faire flèche*.

130. Je vous *prends au mot*, à une condition.

131. J'ai bien peur qu'elle *aille au devant d'*une désillusion.

132. Je vois bien qu'elle est en retard, mais servez le déjeuner, elle nous *rattrapera*.

133. Est-ce que tu vas *donner raison à* ta fille ?

134. *D'ici un an* tout cela sera changé.

135. Il est *de toute nécessité* que tous les deux soient là.

136. Il m'a avoué *se sentir à l'étroit* rue Castille.

137. Faire suivre.
     (—*Indication sur une enveloppe.*)

138. Au suivant !

139. Je donnerais *tout au monde pour* apprendre à danser comme lui.

140. Ne va donc pas *te creuser la tête* pour savoir ça.

141. Le silence ! Mais, mon ami, c'est le pire ennemi de l'amour !

142. *Depuis dix mois que* j'ai fini le traitement je n'ai pas *repris de poids*.

143. Il a plu. Le ciel est encore *bas* et toujours *encombré*.

129. I'm at my wits' end.

130. I take you at your word, on one condition.

131. I'm greatly afraid she is in for a disillusion.

132. I see well enough she is late, but bring in luncheon, she will catch us up.

133. Are you going to back your daughter up (take her part)?

134. A year hence all that will be changed.

135. It's absolutely necessary both should be there.

136. He confessed to me that he felt a bit cramped in the Rue Castille.

137. Please forward.
     (—*Marked on an envelope.*)

138. Next, please!

139. I'd give anything in the world to learn to dance like him.

140. Don't go worrying your head to find that out.

141. Silence! But, my friend, that's the worst enemy of love!

142. Since finishing the treatment ten months ago I've not put on any weight.

143. It's been raining. The sky is still clouded and lowering.

144. La jeune fiancée a neuf ans *de moins que* son *époux*.

NOTE— *Un époux :*

        Une épouse :

        Les époux :

        Un marié :

        Une mariée :

        Les mariés :

145. Je crains que cette pièce ne *fasse* pas *long feu*.

146. Je passe mon temps *de mon mieux*.

147. Le service des vedettes est suspendu. Il va *reprendre* à 3 h.

148. —Quand commence-t-on ?
—Mais quand vous voud*rez !*

149. Je n'y *puis rien*.

150. Je n'en *puis mais*.

151. Je n'en *puis plus*.

152. On ne *peut rien*, *aux* faits accomplis, que d'en tirer, courageusement, la leçon. (—*La Garçonne, roman par V. Margueritte publié en 1922*.)

144. The young fiancée is nine years younger than her betrothed.

     NOTE—*Un époux* may be: betrothed, bridegroom, or husband.

     Une épouse may be: betrothed, bride, or wife.

     Les époux means 'husband and wife'; 'Mr and Mrs —.'

     Un marié is a bridegroom (after the ceremony).

     Une mariée is a bride (after the ceremony).

     Les mariés means 'married people.'

145. I'm afraid this play will hang fire (go badly).

146. I pass my time as best I can.

147. The ferry-boat service is hung up. It starts again at 3 p.m.

148. —When do we begin?

     —Why, whenever you like!

149. I can't help it.

150. I've nothing to do with it (am not responsible for it).

151. I'm done up (can do no more).

152. You can't do anything with accomplished facts, except learn a lesson from them, bravely. [*From the novel La Garçonne ('the flapper')*]

153. Avez-vous reçu les nouv*eaux disques ?*

154. Il sait bien de quoi *il retourne.*

155. J'ai failli chiper une contravention.
(*pron.* con-tra-van-si-on.)

156. Elle le quittait régulièrement sur le seuil
(*pron.* seu-ll) de sa porte avec un baiser,
*pour peu qu'*elle fut de bonne humeur.*
* *Pour peu que...* here is equivalent to *si peu que...*
Pour peu que, meaning 'if only,' requires following
verb in the subjunctive.

157. Comment *se fait-il* que vous êtes *si peu
nombreux ?*

158. Les autres l'ont un peu *battu froid.*

159. Pour chasser dans ce pays, il vous faut un
bon sauteur, *râblé,* solide, l'arrière-main
puissante, l'épaule sortie, de l'encolure. Faut
avoir quelque chose devant soi !

160. Au Concours Hippique, cette année,
le comble de raffinement a été, pour les
amazones, d'assortir leurs robes aux *robes*
de leurs *montures.*

161. Moi, vous savez, *un rien* m'habille !

162. —Est-ce que j'*y suis pour quelque chose ?*
—Plutôt ! répondit-il.

163. Je ne voudrais pas *faire des potins.*

153. Have you got the new (gramophone) records?

154. He knows quite well what is up.

155. I just escaped copping a summons.

156. She left him regularly on her doorstep with a kiss, however little good-humoured she was.

157. How is it there are so few of you?

158. The others treated him a bit coolly (rather cold-shouldered him).

159. To hunt in this country, you must have a good fencer, well ribbed-up, sturdy, with powerful quarters, free shoulders, and a good forehand. Must have something in front of you!

160. At the Horse Show, this year, the last word in refinement was, for the lady-riders, to match their habits with the colour of their mounts' coats.

161. You know, I can dress on a mere nothing!

162. —Have I got anything to do with it?
    —Rather! he replied.

163. I shouldn't like to talk tittle-tattle.

164. Il a tout *à l'œil.*

165. Je suis désolé de vous avoir *fait rencontrer avec* des personnes qui vous déplaisent.

166. La question du *chômage* devient sérieuse. Il faut assister les *sans-travail.*

167. Le piquet fut précédé *d'*un officier, *sabre au clair.*

168. La sentinelle en faction donna aussitôt l'alerte *au poste de* garde. Le piquet *d'incendie* arriva.

169. Mais, Madame, que vous a-t-il donc dit ?

170. Elle a lâché la proie pour l'ombre.

171. —J'espère au moins qu'il prendra ses responsabilités.
    —C'est que, justement, j'ai bien peur *que non.*

172. Je viens de dénicher d'admirables *support-chaussettes d'un* nouveau modèle.

173. J'ai égaré mon *blaireau.*

174. Allez vite faire *un brin de* toilette avant le déjeuner.

175. —Vous ne connaissez pas le chemin ?
    —Non, madame, je ne suis pas *d'ici.*

176. Il connaît le turf *dans ses tours et détours.*

164. He gets everything free, gratis, and for nothing.
165. I am distressed at having made you meet people who were objectionable to you.
166. The question of unemployment is becoming serious. It is necessary to assist those out of work.
167. The picquet (picket) was preceded by an officer, with drawn sword.
168. The sentry on duty at once gave the alarm to the guard-room. The fire-picket arrived.

169. But, madame, what did he say to you?

170. She has lost the substance (*lit.* prey) for the shadow.
171. —I hope, at any rate, that he will shoulder his responsibilities.
    —The fact is, I'm greatly afraid he won't.

172. I've just found some splendid sock-suspenders, of a new make.
173. I've mislaid my shaving-brush.

174. Go quick and titivate (make a bit of a toilette; wash up quickly) before lunch.
175. —You don't know the road?
    —No, madame, I am not from these parts.
176. He knows the Turf inside out.

177. Vous me permettrez *de taire son nom*.

178. —Vous ne me *remettez* pas ?
—Mais si—c'est Adèle !

179. *On me paierait que* je ne *voudrais* pas vivre là. C'est à *crever d'*ennui.

180. Nous sommes tous logés à la même enseigne.

181. —Où sont mes *boutons* ?
—Ils ne sont pas dans ta boîte ?
—Mais non, *je ne les trouve pas.*
—Tu as mal cherché, j'y vais... Ils n'y sont pas, en effet. Tu ne les as pas mis ailleurs ?
—Ou voudrais-tu que je les eusse mis ?
—C'est la femme de chambre qui a *dû* les ranger.

182. Il est à vous, ce chien ? Non ? Alors il est *bon pour* la *fourrière*.

183. Nous sommes allés *pendre la crémaillère* chez O—, qui vient de s'installer rue de l'Orient. C'est Yvonne qui nous a traîné là.

184. —Écoute—fit-elle—il est assez difficile de trouver sur-le-champ une situation pour cette petite. Mais en trois jours *je me fais fort de* lui procurer une place.

185. J'ai les nerfs *en pelote*.

177. You must allow me not to mention his (her) name.

178. —You don't remember me?
—Yes I do! it's Adèle!

179. I wouldn't care to live there if I were paid for it. It's enough to kill one with boredom.

180. We are all in the same boat (*lit.* under the same Inn-sign).

181. —Where are my studs?
—Aren't they in your box?
—No, I can't find them.
—You haven't looked properly, I'll have a try ... No, indeed, they are not there. You didn't put them anywhere else?
—Where do you think I'd put them?
—It must have been the maid who tidied them up.

182. Is this dog yours? No? Then he'll have to go to the pound.

183. We went to the house-warming at O—'s place. He's just moved into the rue de l'Orient. 'Twas Yvonne that dragged us there.

184. 'Listen,' she said, 'it's rather difficult to find a situation straight away for this little girl. But inside three days I'll engage to get her a job.'

185. My nerves are all on edge (*lit.* in a pincushion).

186. Vous seriez *si gentille de* nous *faire entendre* quelque chose ?
187. *Ces dames* ne tarderont pas *à* venir.

188. Lisez le *procès-verbal* de la dernière séance.

189. Il *inventoria* la situation.

190. Défronce tes sourcils et ne *t'en fais* pas.

191. Il suffisait qu'un *prétendant* fût *agréé* par elle pour qu'il lui arrivât les pires aventures.

192. Qui la détermine *à rompre avec* une habitude si ancienne ?
193. Il portait des chaussettes *trouées* et *disparates*.
194. Sa jupe *pend* d'un côté.

195. Ces ciseaux sont *émoussés*.

196. Pour atteindre les rayons *haut perchés* il faut vous servir de l'*échelle volante*.
197. Je vous apporte trois *mains* de *papier écolier*. (NOTE— En France, une main de papier est de 25 feuilles.)
198. Elle *gante* du cinq et quart.

199. J'y *aurai l'œil* désormais.

186. Would you be so sweet as to play something for us?
187. The ladies won't be long coming.

188. Read the minutes of the last meeting.

189. He sized up (took stock of) the situation.

190. Stop knitting your brows and don't worry about it.
191. It was quite enough for a suitor to be approved by her, for the worst adventures to befall him.
192. Who is persuading her to break off so old a habit?
193. He was wearing socks (that were) in holes, and not a pair.
194. Her skirt is hanging down one side.

195. These scissors are blunt.

196. You'll have to use the step-ladder to reach the top shelves.
197. I'm bringing you three quires of foolscap paper. (NOTE— The English quire contains twenty-four sheets.)
198. She takes five-and-a-quarter in gloves.

199. I'll keep an eye on it in future (from now on).

200. Je ne l'ai pas revu *de* deux jours.

201. Si seulement nous ne sommes pas pris *par* le brouillard !

202. Je vous assure que nous *n'en menions pas large*.

203. J'avais le *cafard* sans raison.

204. Les enfants *barbotaient* dans les *flaques* de la mer basse.

205. Regardez-moi cet homme *entre deux âges*.

206. Il peut être ignorant ou non, mais *en tout état de cause* il n'a aucune expérience.

207. Ce jeune homme est de bon *naturel*.

208. Je ne veux pas *attacher le grelot pour* le proposer.

209. Ai-je donc la *berlue* ? Je jurerais que j'ai rencontré cette figure-là !

210. Je parle *en connaissance de cause*.

211. Pour *fignoler sa toilette*, Lucie *n'a pas trop d'*une heure !

212. La *traversée est de* quatre heures, et nous en avons déjà *tiré* deux.

213. Nous y trouverons *à qui parler*.

214. À la dernière *manche*, C—, sûr de lui, ne *s'employait* pas.

200. I didn't see him again for two days.

201. I hope we aren't caught in the fog!

202. I assure you we were very near it (only just missed it).

203. For no reason I was in the dumps (blues).

204. The children were paddling (*lit.* dabbling— like ducks) in the puddles at low water.

205. Just look at that middle-aged man.

206. He may be ignorant or not, in any case he has no experience.

207. This young man is good-natured.

208. I don't want to be the first to propose it. (*Attacher le grelot*—to bell the cat.)

209. Are my eyes right, I wonder? I could swear I've seen that face somewhere!

210. I know what I'm talking about.

211. It takes Lucie a good hour to put the finishing touches to her toilette!

212. The crossing (*by sea*) takes four hours, and we've got through two of them already.

213. We'll find someone there to talk to.

214. In the last set (tennis), C—, feeling confident, was not exerting himself.

215. Vous *ferez tant que* pour ne pas avoir l'air de céder, je finirai *par* y aller.

216. Heureusement elle est aussi *casanière* que son mari.

217. Il regardait un gauche dessin, fixé par quatre *punaises* au mur.

218. On aurait juré qu'elle était *de mèche !*

219. Alors, ce n'est qu'un *demi-mal.*

220. Il est bien probable qu'elles *commentent* le prix des bas de soie.

221. *Je ne sors pas de là*, mon ami !

222. Il m'a quitté *sur* une poignée de main.

223. Non, ma chère, l'essayage n'est pas réussi ! Elle est ratée, cette robe. J'y flottais comme une unique *suédoise* dans une boîte d'allumettes !

224. Quand il y en a pour deux, il y en a pour trois.

225. Merci, mon ami, je ne mange pas de ce pain-là !

226. *Mettez-vous en quête d'*un porteur.

227. À bientôt ! Mes bons souvenirs à votre sœur !

215. If you go on like that I shall end up by going there, so as not to look like yielding.
216. Luckily she is as much of a stay-at-home as her husband.
217. He was looking at a clumsy sketch, pinned to the wall by four drawing-pins.
218. One would have sworn she was in the know!
219. Well, then, it might be a lot worse.

220. It's very probable that they are discussing the price of silk stockings.
221. I stick to that (I'm not budging from that), my friend!
222. He left me after shaking hands.

223. No, my dear, the trying-on (fitting) was not a success! That dress has gone all wrong. I was floating about in it like one (Swedish) match left in a match-box!
224. What is enough for two is enough for three.
225. No thanks, my friend, I'm not having anything of that sort! (Expression used when rejecting a proposition one judges not to be quite nice or proper.)
226. Go and look for a porter.

227. So long! Remember me kindly to your sister!

228. D'ailleurs, aurait-elle *un brin raison* ?

229. Elle *est à tu et à toi avec* lui (elle le tutoie).

230. Les hommes très gentils, il y en a des *bottes*. On ne peut savoir ce qu'ils cachent sous leur gentillesse que plus tard, le jour où l'on se dispute pour la première fois.

231. *Quiconque* à Paris *se targue d'*être gourmet connaît la selle d'agneau de chez Viel.*
    C'est à se mettre à genoux devant !
    (* Le Restaurant Viel, à boulevard de la Madeleine à cette époque.)

232. *Pourvu que* le plat *soit* bon, peu importe comment il est fait, mais il faudrait qu'il le soit.

233. Ah ! ma chère, c'est fini ! Je me suis découvert quelques cheveux blancs !

234. Les vieux, avant de *radoter*, sont terriblement sages !

235. Vous m'excuserez si je vous *fausse compagnie ?*

236. *En un mot comme en cent...*

228. Besides, suppose she is right to some extent?

229. She is on the very best of terms with him (sufficiently intimate to use the second person singular).

230. These very kind men, there are heaps (*lit.* bundles) of them (about). You can't tell what they are hiding under their kindness until later on, when you squabble with them for the first time.

231. Everyone in Paris who boasts of knowing good food knows the saddle of lamb at Viel's.* It's a thing to go on one's knees to! (NOTE *[of 1927]*— Let us hope that the new and reconstructed Viel will be as good as the old!)

232. Provided the dish be good, little matter how it be made. But it should be good.

233. Ah! my dear, it's all up! I've found some grey hairs.

234. Old people, before going into their dotage, are terribly wise!

235. You'll forgive me if I leave you?

236. To cut a long story short...

The London Gazette.

Published by Authority.

TUESDAY, NOVEMBER 19, 1907.

BOARD OF AGRICULTURE AND FISHERIES.

Notice is hereby given, in pursuance of section 49 (3) of the Diseases of Animals Act, 1894, that the Board of Agriculture and Fisheries have made the following Orders :—

Date.	Subject.
1907. 9th November	An imported dog belonging to Captain H. T. Russell.
13th November	Dipping of sheep on certain premises in the parish of Kilmuir, Inverness-shire.

Copies of these Orders may be obtained at 4, Whitehall Place, London, S.W.

Il est à vous, ce chien ? Alors il est *bon pour* la *fourrière*.
—Is this dog yours? Then he'll have to go to the pound.

PART IX

CORRESPONDENCE, TITLES & STYLES

LA CORRESPONDANCE, TITRES & QUALITÉS

YOU ARE CERTAIN to have to write letters and send telegrams. If your path lies in high places, you will want to address the Great Ones correctly. Here you will find something about these matters.

LES LETTRES
LETTERS

There is, of course, no end to the possible variations in both style and substance, but it is possible to give some indication of beginnings and endings suitable in various circumstances.

THE DATE

Usually written thus (days and months without a capital):

mardi, le 1er juillet 1927,

or, mardi, le 15 juin 1927,

or (better), mardi, 22 août 1927.

The following abbreviations are occasionally used:

7bre for septembre,

8bre for octobre,

9bre for novembre,

x^{bre} for décembre.

THE BEGINNING AND ENDING

How to begin and end personal, business, and love-letters—

1. Writing to a near relation or an intimate friend, the following forms are permissible:
   > Chère Yvonne,
   >
   > …
   >
   > Je t'embrasse affectueusement, *or*
   > Affectueusement à toi, *or*
   > Ta très dévouée, *or*
   > Ta dévouée,
   > > JEANNE.

   The above is subject to the sex of the writer, and to the propriety of substituting 'vous' for 'toi' etc. where the intimacy is not very close.

2. Writing to an acquaintance of sufficiently long standing, one might put:
   > Cher Monsieur Perrin, Chère Madame, Chère Mademoiselle,
   >
   > …
   >
   > Croyez en mes meilleurs souvenirs, *or*
   > Croyez en ma meilleure sympathie,
   > > JEANNE RIBOT.

3. Writing to a new acquaintance, one might say:
   > Monsieur, Madame, Mademoiselle,
   >
   > …
   >
   > Croyez en mes sentiments distingues,
   > > JEANNE RIBOT.

Or, it may happen that the final words of the text of the letter permit the omission of the formal phrase. *Thus:*

...

J'espère, dès que je serai de retour, profiter de votre aimable invitation.
                    JEANNE RIBOT.

4. Writing to a business establishment, the following forms are usual:

M.M.—et Cie—
Monsieur le Directeur,
Monsieur Richepin,
Madame Saulnier,
Madame Ve (abbr. for *Veuve*) X—,
Messieurs,
Monsieur,
Madame,
...
Veuillez agréer, etc., *(a)* or
Veuillez croire, etc., *(b)* or
Dans l'espoir de vous lire, *(c)*
        JEANNE RIBOT.

(a) meaning: Veuillez agréer l'expression de mes sentiments distingués.

(b) meaning: Veuillez croire à mes sentiments distingués, *or* à mes salutations distinguées.

(c) meaning: Awaiting your reply.

5. A letter *from* a business establishment usually runs thus:

> Mlle Jeanne Ribot,
>
> Nous avons le regret de vous faire connaître …
>
> Veuillez croire, etc.
>
>> Pour le Directeur
>>
>> Le chef de cabinet—LEGROS.

(Surname only, and usually quite illegible!)

6. Writing to a servant, say to one's cook, left in charge of the house, one would simply put:

> Madame Fabre,
>
> …
>
> JEANNE RIBOT.

7. The author does not feel competent to enlighten Bright Young People on the subject of love-letters, beyond suggesting that they are likely to start off by commencing with '*Mon ami* (or *amie*)' and ending with a simple 'Jeanne' or 'Charles.' Then may come '*Chéri* (or *Chérie*),' ending with '*Ta Jeanne*' or '*Ton Charles*.'

It will be much more fun for them to find out for themselves the endless capacity of the French language for terms of endearment! But if they avoid reference to '*tes lèvres*' and '*ta bouche*' the author will be surprised.

L'Adresse de l'enveloppe
Addressing of Envelopes

The normal usages of polite society in England and America are applicable, and there are really no special remarks to make.* It is always well to avoid abbreviating titles—even in the case of a humble Monsieur or Madame. (The abbreviation '*Mons.*' for Monsieur must *never* be used.)

With French provincial addresses, the *Département* should always be indicated, and this is usually abbreviated (*e.g.:* Dinard—*I.-et-V.*, for Ille-et-Vilaine).

Indications in common use are:

FAIRE SUIVRE.— Please forward.

POSTE RESTANTE.— To be called for at the poste restante *guichet*.

Le Timbre de date
Post-mark [1927]

The 'twenty-four-hour' method of timing is in force in the French Post Office, and the normal post-mark [*of 1927 etc.*] reads as follows:

BIARRITZ	(Town etc. P.O.)
21³⁰	(Time marked—9.30 pm)
15–2	(Date—15th February)
27	(Year—1927)
B^ses PYRENEES	(Department)

* NOTE [2010]— A modern preferred standard for the addressing of post[1] is currently provided by *LA POSTE* and the French National Address Management Service (*Service National de l'Adresse*), summarised as follows:

Information to be set out in a specified order, starting with the name of the addressee, on three to six lines maximum (max. seven for international letters), of 38 characters maximum (including spaces) per line; with no punctuation marks or underlining or italics in the 'number and thoroughfare' (*'voie'*) line; with the final 'town/locality' (*'localité'*) line always in capitals [and preferably capitals also for the preceding 'thoroughfare' (*'voie'*) line, and any intervening 'delivery service' (*'lieu-dit'*) line]; and with the address block always justified to the left. The 5-digit postcode (or a Cedex[2] number) appears in the last line in front of the town/locality name.

An individual Cedex[2] code (in place of postcode) is allocated to enterprises which receive large volumes of post, in which case the abbreviation 'CEDEX' is added in capitals after the town/locality name, *e.g.*—

> Alliance française
> 101 boulevard Raspail
> 75270 PARIS CEDEX 06

[1 Variations in addressing envelopes to other French-speaking countries are indicated on page 153 above.]
[2 « *Courrier d'Entreprise à Distribution EXceptionnelle.* »]

Les Télégrammes (*m.*)
Telegrams [of 1927]

Taking the form of a telegram delivered, this may be written out (in the case of smaller offices), or printed in Roman characters by the automatic apparatus in larger offices.

Reading from left to right, the following are the indications preceding the address To—

Office of Origin — Serial No. — No. of Words — Date — Hour of handing in at Office of Origin.

Then follow Service Instructions (if any).

The corresponding French terms are:

Origine — Numéro d'ordre — Nombre de mots — Date — Heure de dépôt — Mentions de service.

The principal service instructions are:

D.	Urgent Telegram.
AR.	Remettre contre reçu, (to be delivered only against a receipt given by addressee).
PC.	Accusé de réception, (acknowledgment of receipt).
RP.	Réponse payée, (reply paid).
TC.	Télégramme collationné, (telegram repeated).

MP.	Remettre en mains propres, (for delivery to addressee personally).
XPx.	Exprès payé, (special delivery fee paid).
Nuit.	Remettre même pendant la nuit, (to be delivered as soon as received, even if during the night).
Jour.	Remettre seulement pendant le jour (only to be delivered during ordinary daytime hours).
Ouvert.	Remettre ouvert, (tél. not to be sealed).

A Cable is Un Câblogramme

La Poste pneumatique
'Pneumatics' [1866-1984*]

In Paris an admirable system of express letter delivery by pneumatic tubes is [was*] in force. Such a letter is familiarly termed *un pneu*, or *un petit bleu*.

They are written on special forms.

* This service, operating through 467 km of pneumatic tubes, commenced in 1866 and opened to the public in 1879, but was discontinued in 1984.

TITRES ET QUALITÉS
Titles and Styles

1. Monsieur, Madame,
   Mademoiselle, etc.

These simple everyday appellations are frequently a stumbling-block to English-speakers, notably as regards pronunciation.

Monsieur.
Monsieur is to be pronounced as if written (in French) *Me-si-eu*. The correct abbreviation is '*M.*'; '*Mons.*' must *not* be used as an abbreviation, the word itself being sometimes employed familiarly or derisively (*and 'Mr.'—a permissable option in 1927—is no longer correct*).

Messieurs (plural) is to be pronounced as if written *Mè-si-eu*. Abbreviation '*MM.*'

Madame.
Madame is all too frequently pronounced *à l'anglaise*, as 'Maddam.' It should be pronounced 'Mah-dahm.' The correct abbreviation is '*Mme*' (or '*Mme*').

Mesdames (plural) should be pronounced 'May-dahm.' The abbreviation is '*Mmes*'.

MADEMOISELLE.

Mademoiselle is often mispronounced 'Maddam-wa-sel.' It should be pronounced as if written (in French) '*Ma-dem-oi-zè-le*,' i.e. 'Ma-demm-wah-zay'l.' The abbreviation is 'Mlle' (or '$Mlle$').

Mesdemoiselles (plural) should be pronounced 'May-demm-wah-zay'l.' Abbreviation 'Mlles'.

[NOTE— '$M.$' and '$MM.$', being truncated at the end, have a full stop *(un point abréviatif)*, while 'Mme', 'Mmes', 'Mlle' etc., being truncated in the middle, have none.]

LE SIEUR, LA DAME, LA FILLE.

In French judicial procedure, the qualifications '*le sieur...*,' '*la dame...*,' '*la fille...*' are often used before proper names instead of *monsieur, madame, mademoiselle. Thus:*

— Vu que le sieur Dupont a déposé de...

— Seeing that Mister Dupont has deposed to ...

MAÎTRE.

The qualification of *maître* (abbreviation 'M^e' (or 'Me'), plural 'MM^{es}') should strictly be confined to *les gens de robe* (members of the legal profession), but enthusiastic or hero-worshipping artistic folk so dub their favourite 'masters' on occasion.

2. SURNAMES / NOMS DE FAMILLE

In French, surnames used in the plural are *invariable* in the following cases:

a. When individuals are indicated.
   E.g.: Les deux Grellet sont nés à Paris.
b. Generally speaking, when ordinary folk are referred to.
   E.g.: Je viens de rencontrer les Smith.
c. When referring to a book or work by the name of its author.
   E.g.: J'ai acheté deux Larousse.

Surnames used in the plural are *variable* when:

a. The words 'people like,' or 'comparable to' are understood.
   E.g.: Les Molières sont rares.
b. Eminent or historical families are referred to.
   E.g.: Les Bourbons.
c. Pictures or works of art are referred to by the name of their painter, etc.
   E.g.: Il a vendu ses Titiens.

The proper names of countries and peoples are *variable*.

NOTE— The French word *surnom* properly means an appellation added to a 'surname,' and is frequently used in the sense of a nick-name (*sobriquet*). A Christian name is un *prénom*, or *un nom de baptême* (*pron.* ba-tème).

3. ROYAL TITLES.

In French the words *empereur, impératrice, roi, reine, prince,* etc., are usually written without a capital, contrary to English usage. A reigning Monarch is addressed as *Votre Majesté* (whether a King or a Queen), or *Sire* (for a King), or *Madame* (for a Queen).

The following abbreviations are used:

S.M.   for *Sa Majesté*
             (His or Her Majesty).
LL.MM.   for *Leurs Majestés*
             (Their Majesties).
S.M.I.   for *Sa Majesté Impériale*
             (His or Her Imperial Majesty).
LL.MM.II. for *Leurs Majestés Impériales*
             (Their Imperial Majesties).

4. Ancient French Royal Titles.

The title of *Dauphin*, borne by the eldest son of the King of France, was first bestowed by Philippe vi of Valois upon his eldest son Jean, afterwards Jean ii, in accordance with one of the conditions of the acquisition (by purchase) of the Province of Dauphiné in 1349. Until then, the title was borne by the suzerain ruler of the territory, which was annexed to France as a set-off against the conquests of the English King Edward iii. The latter monarch had in the same year bestowed upon his eldest son the title of Prince of Wales. (The title of *Dauphin* was inherent in the French King's eldest son, whereas the title of Prince of Wales is not so inherent, but is bestowed at the British Sovereign's discretion in each reign.)

The wife of the *Dauphin* was styled *Dauphine*, and subsequently to the death of Louis xiv the *Dauphin* was addressed and referred to as *Monseigneur* (written with capital).

The next younger brother of the Bourbon Kings was styled *Monsieur* (with capital), and that brother's eldest daughter was styled *Mademoiselle* (with capital).

The title of *Madame* was borne by the daughters of the King, and by the wife of *Monsieur*.

5. SPANISH ROYAL TITLES.

The younger children of the Spanish Sovereign are styled (in Spanish) *Infante* or *Infanta*; in French *Infant*, *Infante*.

6. OTHER ROYAL TITLES.

Princes and Princesses are styled *Altesse Royale* (Royal Highness); *Altesse Sérénissime* (Serene Highness); or *Altesse* (Highness).

The following abbreviations are used:

S.A.R.   for *Son Altesse Royale*
(His or Her Royal Highness).
LL.AA.RR. for *Leurs Altesses Royales*
(Their Royal Highnesses).
S.A.S.   for *Son Altesse Sérénissime*.
LL.AA.SS. for *Leurs Altesses Sérénissimes*.
S.A.   for *Son Altesse*.
LL.AA.   for *Leurs Altesses*.

7. TITLES OF NOBILITY.

The titles of the old French nobility, though suppressed as regards all privileges under the Republican *régime*, are, of course, jealously conserved by their holders, and are used in social intercourse. They are so far recognized by law as to be protected against usurpation by the Penal Code. The several grades, with the English dignities corresponding, are as follows, the French titles (except at the commencement of sentences) being usually written without a capital, which again is contrary to English usage.

Duc (duchesse).	Duke (Duchess).
Marquis (marquise).	Marquess (Marchioness).
Comte (comtesse).	Earl (Countess).
Vicomte (vicomtesse).	Viscount (Viscountess).
Baron (baronne).	Baron (Baroness).
Chevalier (dame).	(No equivalent, and believed by the author to be now extinct as a *French* title).

A *duc* or *duchesse* is styled *Sa Grâce*, referred to as *Sa Grâce le duc (la duchesse) de*—; and addressed as *Votre Grâce*.

A *grand duc* (Russian) is addressed as *Monseigneur*.

Other forms are *monsieur le marquis de* —; *madame la baronne de* —; etc.

The actual use of 'titles' in daily life and social intercourse is regulated much as in England, *i.e.* all depends upon the formality or informality of the occasion, and the degree of intimacy. A casual acquaintance may properly use the ceremonious style that would be quite out of place between friends:

Q.—Mais, madame la baronne, vous ne prenez pas de café ?
R.—Merci, non. Cela empêche monsieur le baron de dormir !

Q.—Why, Baroness! You don't take coffee?
A.—No, thanks. It prevents the Baron from sleeping!

Servants employ the third person of the verb in addressing their masters or mistresses, whether titled or not. *Thus:*

—Quand madame la vicomtesse rentrera, *elle* trouvera le déjeuner tout prêt à servir.
—When *Your* Ladyship returns home, *you* will find luncheon quite ready.

—Quand monsieur voudra, *il* peut l'avoir de chez Z—.
—*You* can get it when you wish, sir, from Z—'s.

Similarly (and here the English usage corresponds) enquiries of, or communications to, servants, relative to their masters or mistresses, are put in the third person. *Thus:*

—Est-ce que madame la comtesse est
  toujours au Touquet ?
—Is Her Ladyship still at Le Touquet ?

—Alors, vous direz à madame qu'on compte
  sur elle pour dîner ce soir.
—Well then, kindly tell madame (your
  mistress) that we are expecting her to
  dinner this evening.

8. AMBASSADORS, MINISTERS.

Ambassadors, Ministers, etc., are styled *Son Excellence* (abbreviation—*S. Exc.*—) and addressed as *Votre Excellence.*

Presidents (of Republican States, of Tribunals, Assemblies, etc.), are simply styled *monsieur le président.*

The several grades of the French *Légion d'Honneur* are:

Grand Officier. (Grand Officer.)
Commandeur. (Commander.)
Officier. (Officer.)
Chevalier. (Knight.)

9. ECCLESIASTICAL TITLES.

The Pope (*Le Pape*) is referred to as *Le Saint Père* (The Holy Father), or *Sa Sainteté* (His Holiness), and addressed as *Votre Sainteté* (Your Holiness).

A Nuncio (*nonce*) or Cardinal (*cardinal*) is referred to as *Son Éminence*, or *Monseigneur*, and addressed as *Votre Éminence*, or *Monseigneur*.

An Archbishop (*archevêque*) or Bishop (*évêque*) is referred to as *Sa Grandeur*, or *Monseigneur*, and addressed as *Votre Grandeur*, or *Monseigneur*.

A Priest is referred to as *le Révérend Père* —, and addressed as *votre révérence* (or simply as *monsieur le curé*, etc.)

A Protestant clergyman is *un pasteur*.

The following abbreviations are used:

Le S.P.	for *Le Saint Père*.
S.S.	for *Sa Sainteté*.
S.Ém.	for *Son Éminence*.
LL.ÉÉm.	for *Leurs Éminences*.
S.G.	for *Sa Grandeur*.
LL.GG.	for *Leurs Grandeurs*.
Le R.P.	for *le Révérend Père*.

10.   Issues of Gender and Person.

The titles and styles of *Majesté, Altesse, Éminence, Excellence, Grâce*, etc., being *feminine in gender*, it follows that pronouns and adjectives used in connection with them must also be feminine, besides agreeing in number. Furthermore, contrary to the English construction, verbs in clauses relating to the title, etc., must be in the *third person. Thus:*

—Si Vos Excellences, tou*tes* surprises qu'*elles* so*ient* d'avoir entendu cette nouvelle, veul*ent* bien *s*'informer de l'affaire, *elles* trouve*ront* que…

—If Your Excellencies, surprised though *you* may be at having heard this news, are good enough to enquire into the matter, *you* will find that…

11. NAVAL AND MILITARY RANKS.

(Note that in French *rank* is not *rang*, but *grade*.) The principal combatant ranks are:

Amiral (*pl.* amiraux).	(Full) Admiral.
Vice-amiral (*pl.* vice-amiraux).	Vice-Admiral.
Contre-amiral (*pl.* contre-amiraux).	Rear-Admiral.
Capitaine de vaisseau.	(Senior) Captain.
Capitaine de frégate.	(Junior) Captain.
Lieutenant de vaisseau.	(Senior) Lieutenant.
Lieutenant de frégate.	(Junior) Lieutenant.
Enseigne.	Midshipman.
Maréchal de France.	Field-Marshal.
Général.	(Full) General.
Général de division.	Lieutenant-General.
Général de brigade.	Major-General.
Colonel.	(Full) Colonel.
Lieutenant-Colonel (*pl.* -s-s).	Lieutenant-Colonel.
Commandant (chef d'escadron, de batterie, de bataillon).	Major (Squadron, Battery, Battalion Commander).
Capitaine.	Captain.
Lieutenant.	Lieutenant.
Sous-lieutenant.	2nd Lieutenant.

Subordinates address their superiors as *'mon général,'* etc., but non-combatant and departmental officers are addressed by their departmental designation, e.g. *'monsieur le vétérinaire.'*

Note that in French *major* is used only in connection with the Medical Service (*médecin-major* ; *médecin-aide-major*, etc.), or as an administrative appellation.

The French equivalent of the phrase 'Officers and Other Ranks' is *'Officiers et Troupe.'*

Officiers généraux comprise all General Officers.

Officiers supérieurs, corresponding to the English 'Field Officers,' include the ranks between *commandant* and *colonel* (both inclusive).

Sous-officiers comprise all non-commissioned officers from the *adjudant* (the senior) to the *maréchal des logis* (in the mounted arms), or the *sergent* (infantry) inclusive. The *brigadier* (in mounted arms) and the *caporal* (infantry) do not rank as *sous-officiers*.

Un gradé is a *brigadier, caporal,* or *sous-officier.*

Un cavalier is a trooper (of cavalry).

Un soldat is a private (of other arms).

Un sapeur is a private soldier of engineers, or a pioneer (of infantry).

The wife of a Field-Marshal, Admiral, General Officer, or Colonel is accorded her husband's style, and may be referred to or addressed as '*madame la colonelle,*' etc.

ÉPILOGUE

Et pour vous, mes chers lecteurs, mes lectrices chéries, j'écris *à la six-quatre-deux* (*pron.* siss-) ce qui me passe par la tête… avec, pour aiguiser l'inspiration, une petite femme peu vêtue sur chaque genou. C'est une légende erronée, quoique *au demeurant* assez flatteuse !

And in your opinion, my dear readers (of both sexes), I write with careless ease and (to aid inspiration) a scantily-clad damsel on each knee, just what comes into my head. This idea, though possibly flattering, is quite incorrect.

H—T—R—

STILL BRIGHTER FRENCH

Fin

Photo Gallery

Left and below:
the young H–T–R–

The Cheltenham College rugby xv, 1891
(H–T–R– in back row, third from left)

Photo Gallery

LIEUT.-COL. H. T. RUSSELL,
AROUND 1920

PATRICIA IN THE GARDEN
AT MONTPELLIER, 11 RUE
MOQUIN-TANDON, ~1931

MARION, PATRICIA & HARRY

ACKNOWLEDGEMENTS
Remerciements

THE LIST OF PEOPLE the publishers wish to thank for their help in this project is very long. The search for Harry Thompson Russell went on for years, and a great many individuals went to a lot of trouble to bring it to a successful conclusion.

Two remarkable men were responsible for the sparkling originality of *Brighter French*: its author Harry Thompson Russell, and its illustrator Eric Fraser. The publishers are particularly grateful to the families and copyright holders of them both, whose permissions and help made this book possible.

The personal input of Anne Aston, H–T–R–'s granddaughter, was immense, and the publishers express their profound thanks to her for all the personal effort and time she put into this project, as well as for the information she provided. She not only furnished photographs, sketches, documents and memorabilia of her grandfather, H–T–R–, but also in the course of numerous long telephone conversations, was able to paint a picture of the author as passed on by her mother, Patricia, who remembered a life in which money problems were always present, but there was great family affection. The close relationship between the gentle Patricia, who suffered always from bad health, and H–T–R– comes across clearly in the charming photographs of the two of them taken in France in the 1930s (*page xv*), in which father and daughter gaze at one another with mutual admiration.

The family of Eric Fraser (represented by his son, the Revd Geoffrey Fraser, who also is a trained artist and assisted his father in some of his works) could not have been more generous. Eric Fraser's talent was remarkable—the wit, intelligence and perception of his apparently effortless *Brighter French* drawings making them diamonds among book illustrations. No *roué* was more jaded than Fraser's *roués*, no couturier's *vendeuse* more formidable. The drawings captured and broadcast the oh-so-debunking essence of *Brighter French*, and they undoubtedly played an important part in the book's huge popular success when it was first published.

Many of the drawings in the introductory pages about Eric Fraser appeared first in the BBC *Radio Times*, and one was a stylish fashion drawing for *Harper's Bazaar*. The publishers thank both publications, and the individuals who corresponded with them about the reproduction of these drawings, including Jenny Potter, Managing Editor, BBC Magazines, and Simon Goodman. They also thank the Chris

Beetles Gallery, London, which helped them to make contact with the family of Eric Fraser.

The publishers are extremely grateful to the many people in (or with connections to) Hilperton and Trowbridge in Wiltshire whose efforts to help them track down H–T–R– were nothing short of heroic. Their first contact was with Elaine Shepherd, who now owns part of Southfield House in Hilperton, where the Russells lived between 1946 and 1953. Mrs Shepherd could not find information about H–T–R–, but provided recent history of the property and the name and address of the previous owner, Frank Holgate of Lancashire. Mr Holgate also had no personal knowledge of H–T–R–, but in his turn, he contacted Conny Parrott, who had worked for a time for Mr Pilkington, the owner of Southfield prior to Mr Holgate. Ms Parrott kindly made numerous enquiries, and came up with the names of two very helpful contacts, Glynn Bridges at the Civic Centre in Trowbridge, and Ken Rogers, retired County Archivist. When Mr Rogers was unable to find any new information in local records, he made the suggestion that finally led to a breakthrough: i.e. that the publishers should write a letter to the *Wiltshire Times*. The publishers thank its editor, Neville Smith, for publishing the letter, which was seen by a surprised Anne Aston, who immediately made contact.

Also in Wiltshire, Catrina Saunders, head gardener at The Courts in Holt, provided fascinating information about the period when H–T–R– was head gardener there in the 1940s. The photograph of the gardener's cottage (where Catrina lives now) was taken by Kaye Haworth.

The publishers very much appreciate the help given to them by Cheltenham College and its archivist, Christine Leighton. Mrs Leighton provided information about H–T–R–'s studies and prizes won by him at Cheltenham College, as well as the photograph of the school's 1891 rugby team, which included H–T–R–. That photograph, as well as the very informative extracts from the Cheltenham College Register, are reproduced by the kind permission of the college.

For their help in the search for H–T–R–, the publishers sincerely thank J. D. Jenkins of the British Library Humanities Reference Service; Paul Evans, librarian of the Royal Artillery Museum at Woolwich; Margaret Harrison, archivist, Strathclyde University; Norman Paget, honorary British Consul at Montpellier; *la Mairie de Montpellier*; Georges Patrone of the *Archives départementales de l'Hérault*; M.

Merle (of the *Cadastre* at Montpellier); & Frédéric Charpenet of H–T–R–'s 1930s address in Montpellier.

Other individuals and institutions for whose input and/or resources the publishers are extremely grateful include: John Russell (H–T–R–'s grandson) of County Cork; Claire Bourgeois, *directrice, Alliance française* Dublin; *l'Imprimerie nationale de France*; Ann Mitchell, archivist, Bedford Estates, Woburn; the Little Company of Mary and the Milford Care Centre, and George Lee (for his photographs of H–T–R–'s boyhood home, Milford House, Limerick); John Draisey, County Archivist, Devon Record Office; Trinity College Library, Dublin; the National Library of Ireland; *Burke's Irish Family Records*; the U.K. National Archives, Kew; the National Archives of Ireland; the Royal United Services Institute, Whitehall; the U.K. Office of Public Sector Information and the *London Gazette* which published the mentions in Despatches and other official announcements concerning H–T–R–, his family and (on one occasion, *page 256*) his dog.

SOURCES

The Search for H—T—R—

Most of the photographs relating to H–T–R– (and the Boer War sketch and business card) on pages xii to xxiii, 256, 282 & 283 were provided by, and are reproduced by kind permission of, H–T–R–'s grand-daughter Anne Aston. Three photographs are from other sources, on pages— xii (in excerpt) & 282 (in full):

> The 1891 school rugby team photograph is from Cheltenham College Archives, and reproduced by kind permission of the college.

xiii   The view of Milford House, Limerick, is based on photographs taken by George Lee.

xvi   The view of the cottage at The Courts, Holt, taken by Kaye Haworth, was provided by Catrina Saunders, Head Gardener, The Courts.

Eric Fraser

Eric Fraser's original 1927 drawings for *Brighter French* are on the cover (and frontispiece) and on pages 18, 26, 154, 194 & 216 (with excerpts on pages 1, 98 & 281).

Two additional Fraser drawings are included in this edition: 'American in Paris' on page 2, first published in BBC *Radio Times* in 1931; and 'Father I have sold a drawing' on page 62, which originally illustrated a 1926 article by his agent R.P. Gossop in *Commercial Art* magazine.

Acknowledgements & Sources

The inset Fraser drawings illustrating his biography (on pages xxv to xxxiii) are:

PAGE

xxv   Jacket & frontispiece illustration for *Brighter French*, pen-and-ink, 1927.

xxvi   'The Ballad of John Axon,' pen-and-ink, *Radio Times* 27 June 1958.

xxvii   Portrait of the artist's grandmother, watercolour, 1922.

xxviii   'Old and New World,' pen-and-ink, *Harper's Bazaar*, 1929.

xxix   [also on page 2] 'American in Paris,' pen-and-ink, *Radio Times* 24 July 1931.

xxx   'Milner Gray' (aka 'Hunting-crop Gray') pen-and-ink, 1928.

xxxi   'Night Flight,' pen-and-ink, *Radio Times* 3 April 1942.

xxxii   'St Michael,' stained glass, 1963, in Church of Saint Mary the Virgin, Hampton-on-Thames.

xxxiii   Self-portrait, ink and charcoal, 1949.

The sources for indexed references to published works quoted within the Fraser biography (pages xxv to xxxiii) are as follows:

REF.

1   Alec Davis, *The Graphic Works of Eric Fraser* (The Uffculme Press, Dalvey House, Great Malvern, 1974 & 1985), p. 2.

2   Silvia Backemeyer, *Eric Fraser Designer & Illustrator* (Lund Humphries Publishers, Russell Gdns, London, 1998), p. 22, citing—
RD Usherwood, *Drawing for Radio Times*, 1961.

Acknowledgements & Sources

3   Backemeyer, *Eric Fraser Designer &c.*, p. 8, citing—
    John Barmas, *Men of Vision no. 7: Eric Fraser—Sickert didn't influence him,* 1953.
4   Backemeyer, p. 8, citing—
    Francis Marriott, letter of reference of June 1927.
5   Davis, *The Graphic Works &c.*, page v.
6   Backemeyer, p. 11, citing—
    Wᵐ Johnstone, *Points in Time: An Autobiography,* 1980.
7   Backemeyer, p. 11.
8   Davis, p. 15.
9   Davis, page iv.
10 Backemeyer, p. 22.
11 Davis, p. 22.
12 Davis, pp. 25-26.

London Gazette Excerpt (page 256)

An excerpt from the *London Gazette* of 19th November 1907 is reproduced on page 256 by licence of the UK Office of Public Sector Information. The 'imported dog' (brought from South Africa by H–T–R–) is portrayed by Ella, who belongs to Susan Aston, H–T–R–'s great-granddaughter.

NOTES

In these new editions of *Brighter French* and its companion volumes *The Brighter French Word-Book* and *Still Brighter French*, French text and English text have been typeset individually in accordance with the different punctuation and typographical rules/conventions which apply for each language.

Also in these 2010-2012 editions, a small number of original (1927-1932) French abbreviations are adjusted, as follows—

To correspond with modern usage, 'F' or 'francs' are used in place of 'frs.' 'fr.' & 'fcs.' (as were in the original editions); similarly, 1re and 2e are used in place of 1ère and 2me, and 'M.' in place of 'M^r' (*'monsieur'*).

Where, in the original books, em-dashes [rather than quotation marks or *guillemets (« »)*] were used in both languages to denote conversation, these have been retained.

The BRIGHTER FRENCH WORD-BOOK
—A Guide to 'the Right Word' for Bright Young People
by Harry Thompson RUSSELL

352 pages, 32 illustrations
ISBN (PBK.): 978-0-9553756-99

Volume II in the classic
Brighter French Series,
written in the 1920s for 'Bright
Young People who already know some'

Vocabulary on a wide range of
subjects—both of universal interest—
   the House, the Town, Illness, the Weather, etc.
and more specialised—
   Horses, Firearms and Target Shooting, Finance and
   Business, Nautical Matters, etc.
with distinctions that are hard to find in a dictionary.

'…remarkable for the amazing detail that is presented.
The Motoring section would have come in handy many
years ago when I broke down in France. …Television
and computers make no appearance, of course, but just
about everything else is present in this handy paperback.'
—ELSEVIER *SYSTEM* JOURNAL [2010], ROBERT VANDERPLANK
DIRECTOR, LANGUAGE CENTRE, UNIVERSITY OF OXFORD

'It is a book unique of its kind, and if anybody who has
occasion ever to speak French is content to do without
it, then he is either a perfect French scholar—or else
very conceited!' —*TRUTH MAGAZINE* [1929]

PHAETON PUBLISHING LTD. DUBLIN WWW·PHAETON·IE

STILL BRIGHTER FRENCH
—for Bright Young People (who now know more)
by Harry Thompson RUSSELL

illustrated with the
works of Emil VAN HAUTH

330 pages, 20 illustrations
(in colour and b+w)
ISBN (PBK): 978-0-9561055-16

Volume III in the classic
Brighter French Series

53. 'I don't mean to say
that you never see
married people there,
only they're not
married to one another.'

53. « Je ne veux pas
dire qu'on n'y voit
pas de gens mariés,
mais ils ne sont pas
mariés ensemble. »

377. 'He must have quite
a lot to say! The less
people do, the more
they have to talk about.'

377. « Il doit *en avoir à*
dire ! *Moins* les gens
en font, et plus ils en
ont à rencontrer. »

'…H-T-R- doesn't just want you to parrot French phrases,
the essential of fluent speech is to think as the French do. …'
—ELSEVIER *SYSTEM* JOURNAL [2010], ROBERT VANDERPLANK
DIRECTOR, LANGUAGE CENTRE, UNIVERSITY OF OXFORD

'*Brighter French*— when you start to read you giggle.
This naughty guide to flappers' French is full of useful
phrases. …' —*EVENING HERALD*, Dublin, [2011]

PHAETON PUBLISHING LTD. DUBLIN WWW·PHAETON·IE

The Secret of Jules and Josephine
—An Art Deco Fairy Tale
by Artemesia D'Ecca

400 pages, 22 drawings
ISBN (PBK): 978-0-9553756-20

Set in modern times and in
1927 France & U.S.

'... impressive and imaginative ...'
—*INIS* MAGAZINE

'... A wonderful book ... it is for all
ages ... Irish fairies flying all over Opéra Paris ... magic,
time-travel, comedy, mystery ... Irish fairies are the
best!' —BRENTANO'S, PARIS

'While sending a strong but subtle environmental
message, the book evokes the swinging lifestyle of 1920s
Paris, as well as life on board an ocean liner of the period,
with a fair smattering of latter-day celebrities like F. Scott
Fitzgerald, Charles Lindbergh, Charlie Chaplin, Coco
Chanel and Sigmund Freud, who all help the fairies "at
their time of greatest need." ... It is all great fun, and
cleverly done.' —*BOOKS IRELAND*

'... I think anyone who read her book would start
believing in fairies. I've always believed in them. My
favourite character was Fuchsia. I liked it very much ...'
—EMILY SCHOFIELD (AGE 11), MUNICH

PHAETON PUBLISHING LTD. DUBLIN WWW·PHAETON·IE

Also from Phæton Publishing

Extremely Entertaining Short Stories
—Classic Works of a Master
by Stacy AUMONIER

576 pages: biography, 29 stories, 1 essay
ISBN (PBK): 978-0-9553756-37
ISBN (HBK): 978-0-9553756-51

Stories of World War I & the
1920s in England & France

'Stacy Aumonier is one of the
best short story writers of all time.
His humour is sly and dry and
frequent ... And can't he write!'
—JOHN GALSWORTHY (winner of Nobel Prize for Literature).

'... a very elegant volume ... short stories that invite
comparison with those of Saki, O. Henry and even Guy
de Maupassant.' —*BOOKS IRELAND*

Broadcast on BBC RADIO 4 *Afternoon Readings* in 2011.

'... in England, my first trip there in 25 years ... I bought
the new Phaeton collection of *Extremely Entertaining
Short Stories* by Stacy Aumonier ... greatly appreciated
in his time for his wit and neatly contrived plots. Back
now in New York, it's a heavy volume to cart back and
forth as subway reading, but it's well worth the weight!'
—*LIBRARY JOURNAL*, NEW YORK

'... a great holiday read.' —BRENTANO'S, PARIS

'...I suspect there will be many readers, young and
old, who will warmly welcome this collection by an
accomplished writer...' —*THE IRISH CATHOLIC*, 2012

PHAETON PUBLISHING LTD. DUBLIN WWW·PHAETON·IE